The New Pacific Community

The New Pacific Community

U.S. Strategic Options in Asia

Martin L. Lasater

WestviewPress

A Division of HarperCollinsPublishers

Copyright © 1996 by Westview Press, Inc., A Division of HarperCollins Publishers, Inc.

Published in 1996 in the United States of America by Westview Press, Inc., 5500 Central Avenue, Boulder, Colorado 80301-2877, and in the United Kingdom by Westview Press, 12 Hid's Copse Road, Cumnor Hill, Oxford OX2 9JJ

A CIP catalog record for this book is available from the Library of Congress
ISBN 0-8133-8869-4

The paper used in this publication meets the requirements of the American National Standard for Permanence of Paper for Printed Library Materials Z39.48-1984.

10   9   8   7   6   5   4   3   2   1

To my children

Zara, Keyne, Kieran, Chryseis, Kendrik, and Kalon

Contents

Introduction

U.S. strategy toward the Asian-Pacific region is important because the Pacific Rim is of vital and growing concern to the United States. Four major power centers interact in the Asia-Pacific: the United States, Japan, Russia, and China. A fifth power center, India, is emerging in southern Asia. The Asian-Pacific region has the world's largest standing armies in close proximity to each other, and the dangers of war in Korea and conflict in the Taiwan Strait and South China Sea are palpable. Half of U.S. aircraft carrier battle groups and amphibious forces are oriented toward the Pacific Ocean, the largest military theater in the world.

With the end of the Cold War, national security has become not merely a military concern but an economic issue as well. In that regard, no region is more important to vital U.S. interests than the Asian Pacific. The region is the world's fastest growing economy, producing about 35 percent of total world trade and, together with the United States, half of the world's gross national product. The Pacific Rim is the largest U.S. trading partner, accounting for nearly 55 percent of global U.S. trade, about 50 percent of total U.S. exports, and 60 percent of total U.S. imports. Exports to Asia provide more than two million American jobs.

The growing military and economic power of Asia is creating a tripolar world comprising the Americas, Europe, and Asia. The United States needs an effective strategy toward the region to serve its security, political, economic, and cultural interests. These interests cannot be served adequately through bilateral relations, benign neglect, or nonengagement. The United States must devise a viable strategy toward Asia because it is in the U.S. interest to be engaged actively in the region and to influence its direction.

The purpose of this book is to examine U.S. strategic options toward the Asian-Pacific region for the remainder of this century. The book's focus is on the strategies, not their authors. Nor is there an attempt to be exhaustive. Great effort has been made, however, to define an operable range of strategies available to the United States for the next five to ten years.

Chapter 1, "The Bush Legacy in Asia," provides a brief overview of U.S. global and regional strategies during the Cold War. It then turns to a more detailed examination of President George Bush's efforts to define a new strategy "beyond containment" and to create a "new world order" comprised of a community of market democracies. Strategies of "collective engagement" and "regional contingencies" are discussed, the 1992 Joint Military Net Assessment is reviewed, and Bush's strategy and policy toward Asia are examined. The East Asia strategic initiative (EASI-I and EASI-II) reports are analyzed.

Chapter 2, "Principles of Clinton Foreign Policy," discusses President Bill Clinton's foreign policy and national security strategy. "Engagement" is explained, as well as the administration's "three pillars" of economic growth, military strength, and support for democracy. The strategic aspects of "assertive multilateralism," "enlargement," and the "bottom-up review" are also examined in detail.

Chapter 3, "The New Pacific Community," reviews Clinton's strategy and policy toward Asia. Ten U.S. policy goals are summarized, as well as "five building blocks" of the Pacific community. U.S. policies toward the Asia-Pacific Economic Cooperation (APEC) process and the North Korean nuclear weapons program are cited as examples of how Clinton's regional strategy was implemented. The U.S. Pacific Command strategy of "cooperative engagement" is examined, as well as definitive administration policy statements through 1995. The 1995 East Asian strategic initiative report (EASI-III) also is discussed.

Chapter 4, "USCINCPAC Studies," examines four publicly released strategic forecasts sponsored by the U.S. Pacific Command during the 1989-1992 period. Two were prepared by the Strategic Planning and Policy Directorate at USCINCPAC headquarters in Hawaii, and two were written for the USCINCPAC by the Rand Corporation of Santa Monica, California, a think-tank frequently contracted by the Department of Defense. The four studies represent transitional strategies from the post-containment era, bridging the Cold War and post-Cold War periods. All emphasize the multifaceted roles played by the U.S. military in the Asia-Pacific region.

Chapter 5, "Alternative Strategies," considers a number of options from nongovernmental sources organized according to major themes of deterrence, balance of power, emerging threats such as China, collective security, multilateralism, isolationism, and integration. These strategic proposals, taken from the 1991-1995 period, present a wide range of possible approaches for the United States as it interacts with Asia over the next several decades.

The concluding Chapter 6 summarizes the strategic options discussed in the book and makes several recommendations for future U.S. strategy toward the Asian Pacific. Briefly, these recommendations include:

- The United States needs to have an effective regional strategy toward the Asia-Pacific.
- The strategy needs to be robust and comprehensive, including close coordination between military, political, economic, and cultural elements, and be directed by effective leadership in Washington.
- The role of the U.S. military in Asian-Pacific strategy is vital, but security in Asia must be defined beyond military terms.
- U.S. strategy should have as one of its goals the maintenance of a favorable balance of power in Asia, but such a regime should not be the predominant feature of U.S. strategy.
- U.S. strategy should not be based on either cooperative or hostile relations with Beijing, as Sino-American relations will remain in a state of flux for some time.
- The U.S.-Japan alliance should remain the linchpin of American strategy toward the Asian Pacific.
- U.S. strategy toward Asia in the post-containment period should contain strong elements of collective security and multilateralism, but the United States must retain the ability to act unilaterally when necessary.
- American strategy toward Asia will be influenced by tendencies toward isolationism in the United States.
- Integration should become a more prominent feature of U.S. strategy toward the Asian Pacific and perhaps its defining characteristic in the near future.

I wrote this book in the hope that it would stimulate study and debate over what comprises an effective U.S. strategy toward Asia. The region is too important to ignore and too large to permit easy assessment. I welcome your comments and suggestions, and I look forward to our continued dialogue on this vital subject.

1

The Bush Legacy in Asia

From the outset of its relations with Asia, the United States has been concerned with security, trade, and cultural expansion.[1] During the Cold War, however, the dominant U.S. concern focused on the security threat from communism. The primary U.S. strategy to contain communism was "extended deterrence."[2] Formulated during the Korean War, the term usually referred to the application of American military power, both nuclear and conventional, to guarantee the security of U.S. allies from external attack by positioning U.S. forces at the point of the expected initial conflict, thus preventing the outbreak of war in the first place and precluding its escalation to global levels. In practice, the term meant any defense alliance with the United States, regardless of the number of U.S. troops forward deployed in that country.

The strategic rationale of extended deterrence was that by forming a series of treaties and commitments with regional friends and allies (most importantly in Western Europe, the Middle East, and the Asian-Pacific rim), the United States could present to the Soviet Union or other potential hostile powers a formidable deterrent and a stronger collective defense should deterrence fail. In the case of the Soviet Union (the only country capable of mounting a global threat to the United States), the combined strength of extended deterrence was stronger than the sum of its parts because the alliances formed a multitude of potential fronts around the USSR that would be impossible for Moscow to engage.

President Harry Truman's global deterrence strategy was shaped by NSC-68, which concluded that the Soviet Union had sufficient conventional forces to overwhelm Western Europe and would soon deploy sufficient nuclear weapons to deter U.S. intervention. This assessment, coupled with the fall of China in 1949 and the outbreak of the Korean War in 1950, prompted the Truman administration to undertake a large-scale buildup of American conventional and nuclear forces.

By late 1953 the United States had sufficiently rearmed to the point where it could overcome any conventional force in Europe and Asia. President Eisenhower accordingly authorized a "New Look" at U.S. deterrence strategy so as to better balance American commitments and available resources. The product was NSC 162/2, which formalized the "New Look" strategy of massive retaliation.

President Kennedy added another dimension to U.S. deterrence strategy with his "flexible response." This was an attempt to prepare the United States to respond to a wider spectrum of general and limited wars at all levels of conflict. In the early 1970s President Nixon mandated yet another shift in strategy, from being able to fight "two-and-a-half" wars simultaneously to "one-and-a-half" wars. The Nixon Doctrine also limited U.S. military intervention except in cases of clear commitment. President Carter sustained the "one-and-a-half" deterrent strategy but required that allies accelerate their own defense expenditures and force buildups within the framework of their security alliances with the United States.

The Reagan administration reversed the trend of reducing U.S. defense commitments begun under Nixon and continued under presidents Ford and Carter. Reagan embarked on a massive rearmament, emphasizing the need for extended deterrence to enhance global stability. This continued until 1985, when defense expenditures began to decline in real terms. By 1988 developments in the Soviet Union had reached the point where Reagan said that the monolithic threat from communism underlying U.S. deterrence strategies was no longer valid and that a new, more complex, and "discriminate" deterrence should be adopted. Discriminate deterrence took into account not only military factors but socioeconomic and cultural variables as well. This was made necessary because the United States was no longer economically dominant and it could not afford to extend a deterrent against every potential threat to U.S. global interests.

For much of the post-World War II period, the most fundamental American national security interest in the Asian Pacific was to incorporate the region into an international order as an independent center of power and stability, while preserving U.S. access to its resources and markets and precluding its geopolitical subjugation by a power or coalition of powers hostile to the United States.[3] The U.S. strategy of extended deterrence was a cost-efficient way to do this, while at the same time allowing American friends and allies to develop economically and politically. In the immediate postwar period, Washington felt the newly independent Asian nations would move toward democracy rather than authoritarianism, facilitating the region's pursuit of free, market-based trade -- all of which would be in the U.S. interest.

An intermediate strategic task developed over time: achieving an acceptable regional balance of power. This required the United States to control Pacific sea lines of communication and to maintain its position as a major political influence in the region. It also required the United States to counter the Soviet Union's power projection capability and to balance the blue water ambitions of other Asian powers such as China, Japan, and India. Alliance or coalition strategy served the latter purpose, and the development of regional and subregional defense communities, such as cooperation with the Association of Southeast Asian Nations (ASEAN), helped as well.

By extension, other U.S. strategic interests evolved: keeping the Japanese and South Korean industrial capabilities on the side of the Western Alliance; maintaining friendly relations with and influence in China; protecting the flow of commercial and military traffic through Southeast Asian waters; and keeping other powers from meddling in the Pacific island-states.

During the Cold War, the United States generally saw the Asian-Pacific region in terms of global strategy rather than as a separate strategic arena. The same deterrence criteria applied to Europe and the Middle East were applied as well to Asia, including flexible response, escalation control, forward deployments, and force sustainability. This was done, despite the fact that Asian nations were not likely to face a global threat. Threats to Asian nations were primarily from distinct and unique sources from within their own region.

The New World Order

When President George Bush entered office in January 1989, he emphasized the need for the United States to use key technologies, weapons systems, and operational concepts to maximize the deterrent value of U.S. forces, increasingly constrained due to limited resources.

Within a few months of his administration, however, it became obvious that the Soviet Union no longer posed a global threat to the United States. Bush therefore began the search for a new U.S. national security strategy, one "beyond containment."

The Bush administration was confronted with fundamental shifts in the international environment. These included the bankruptcy of communism, worldwide economic integration heightened by technological change, and global movements toward market-oriented economies and political pluralism. These trends were welcomed by the United States, because they were considered to be the realization of American goals held since the end of World War II.

But there were significant problems for the United States as well. Of special concern were a reemergence of ethno-nationalism, regional antagonisms, and ambitions held in abeyance because of the Cold War. Modern weaponry fueled local antagonisms. There were also basic contradictions in the international environment which greatly complicated U.S. national security policy: power was becoming more diffuse between nations, even as they were becoming more interdependent; the technological and information revolutions were eroding national boundaries, yet nationalism was becoming a more powerful force in the world; technological and commercial capabilities were becoming more important than military capabilities in determining the power of nations; but advanced weapons, including weapons of mass destruction, were proliferating at alarming rates.

To conceptualize a new international system that would replace the bipolar world of the Cold War, Bush expressed support for a "new world order" reflecting American values and long-term national objectives. At the graduation ceremony of the Coast Guard Academy in New London, Connecticut, on May 24, 1989, Bush defined his goal: "What is it that we want to see? It is a growing community of democracies anchoring international peace and stability, and a dynamic free-market system generating prosperity and progress on a global scale. The economic foundation of this new era is the proven success of the free market -- and nurturing that foundation are the values rooted in freedom and democracy."[4] The creation of this new world order became the predominant theme of U.S. foreign policy through the end of 1995.

The first major test of Bush's commitment to the new world order came in August 1990, when Iraq invaded Kuwait. Acting deliberately and only after being assured of both international and domestic support, Bush ordered massive American military forces into the Persian Gulf region. In explaining his actions, Bush said one of his main reasons for military intervention in the Gulf was to protect the new world order.[5]

The minor role played by Moscow in the Persian Gulf crisis and the overwhelming power projection capabilities displayed American forces confirmed that the United States was the world's only superpower. Despite the enthusiasm accompanying the U.S. victory, which briefly led to calls for an extended Pax Americana, there were at least three factors contributing to the success of Desert Storm.

1. The key role played by the U.S. military, including its sophisticated weapons systems and unique power projection capabilities.
2. The substantial international political support given the U.S. effort, including a large coalition of nations supporting United Nations' resolutions against Iraq.[6]
3. The enormous financial contribution made to the war effort by other nations.[7]

For a time, the U.S.-led coalition victory over Iraq increased support for the new world order. In his State of the Union address on January 29, 1991, Bush said the United States was in the Persian Gulf to defend the new world order in which diverse nations would work together for the universal aspirations of "peace and security, freedom, and the rule of law."[8] A few weeks later on March 6, 1991, Bush told a Joint Session of Congress that he saw the war as the first test for the "new world order...in which freedom and respect for human rights find a home among all nations."[9]

The president delivered a major speech on the new world order at Maxwell Air Force Base on April 13, 1991.[10] Comparing the end of the Cold War to the end of the first and second world wars, Bush noted that each of confrontations had given birth to a dream of a world in which major powers worked together to ensure peace. Bush said he did not have a specific "blueprint" in mind that would govern the conduct of nations or some supernational structure or institution which would manage the new world order. Nor did the new world order mean surrendering national sovereignty or forfeiting national interests. Rather, the new world order referred to "new ways of working with other nations to deter aggression and to achieve stability, to achieve prosperity and, above all, to achieve peace."

According to Bush, the new world order was based on a shared commitment between nations to a common set of principles. These principles included "peaceful settlements of disputes, solidarity against aggression, reduced and controlled arsenals, and just treatment of all peoples." The quest for a new world order was, in part, "a challenge to keep the dangers of disorder at bay."

Bush said the new world order "gains its mission and shape not just from shared interests, but from shared ideals." The United States was the home for these ideals. Bush said: "The ideals that have spawned new freedoms throughout the world have received their boldest and clearest expression in [the United States]. What makes us American is our allegiance to an idea that all people everywhere must be free."

The quest for a new world order became less popular during the last two years of the Bush administration, as intractable and brutal struggles arose in the former Yugoslavia, Somalia, and elsewhere. Expectations that the post-Cold War period would be one of peace and stability proved overly optimistic. President Bush found himself severely criticized for concentrating too much on international affairs and failing to improve the U.S. economy. Nonetheless, the broad themes of the new world order reemerged with greater clarity under the Clinton administration, particularly in its goals to enlarge the community of market democracies and build a new Pacific community.

Collective Engagement

Concerned that foreign policy would be relegated to such a low priority that the United States would lose its influence in world affairs, Secretary of State James Baker provided a key rationale for a continued American leadership role in a speech before the Chicago Council on Foreign Relations in April 1992.[11] Noting that the United States had been called upon to lead the world into a peaceful new order following the first and second world wars, Baker said a new call was being heard after the Cold War. The United States decided to stay out of world affairs after World War I, but the disasters of isolationism, which included the Great Depression and the rise of dictatorships in Germany and Japan, cost the United States dearly during the Second World War.

After World War II the United States led a forty-year struggle against the communist threat, a struggle which ended with the collapse of the Soviet Union in 1991. Baker recalled that the U.S. decisions to implement the Marshall Plan, to create NATO, and to support democracy in Japan were very controversial. The American people were willing to pay the price of these policies, however, because they understood that containing the Soviet Union was not adequate. The United States had to transform its World War II enemies into democratic friends and allies. The results were what Baker called a "zone of peace and prosperity" in the world.

The end of the Cold War created a third summons for the United States to assume global leadership: this time to win a "democratic peace" for the whole world. According to Baker, "The choice for America is this: We can either try to win this peace through a deliberate policy of working with others to shape our times, or we can stand aside and drift, either out of conviction or neglect, while the times shape us."

The Bush administration wanted to help shape the post-Cold War order by extending the "zone of peace and prosperity" across Russia and Eurasia. "Our idea is to replace the dangerous period of the Cold War with a democratic peace -- a peace built on the twin pillars of political and economic freedom....Shared democratic values can ensure an enduring and stable peace in a way that balance of terror never could, [since] democracies do not go to war with each other."

The administration would attempt to "build a democratic peace by pursuing a straightforward policy of American leadership called `collective engagement.'" Based on U.S. leadership in collaboration with its friends and allies, collective engagement had as its strategic objective the enlargement of the community of market democracies. This collaboration would often occur through the international institutions built after World War II, such as the United Nations, the World Bank, and the International Monetary Fund. However, "the moving force of collective engagement is American leadership, drawing on the common values and common interests shared by the democratic community of nations." U.S. leadership was crucial to "act as the catalyst" in driving forward the expansion of the democratic community. A strategy of collective engagement was possible, Baker said, because "the world trusts us with power...they trust us to do what's right."

The concept of U.S. leadership in a framework of collective engagement "avoids the dangerous extremes of either fallacious omnipotence or misplaced multilateralism." Baker said, "The United States is not the world's policeman. Yet we are not bystanders to our own fate." U.S. action in any given situation would depend on factors such as the nature of the problem, the interests and values at stake, the capacity of U.S. friends to act, and the relevance of available multilateral mechanisms. When necessary, however, the United States would have to act alone "to truly lead or serve our national interests."

As will be seen in the next two chapters, President Bush's vision of a new world order and Secretary Baker's strategy of collective engagement closely paralleled the Clinton administration's strategies of "engagement and enlargement." Although unsuccessful in being reelected for a second term, President Bush firmly established the strategic goals of the United States in the immediate post-Cold War period.

Regional Contingencies and the Base Force

Another continuity between the Bush and Clinton administrations was in the area of national security strategy and military strategy. By 1992 the Bush administration completed an exhaustive reexamination of U.S. strategic options in the post-Cold War period. A fundamental change in national security strategy was made from preparation to fight a global war with Moscow to preparation to fight regional conflicts anywhere in the world. The forces necessary to implement the strategy of regional contingencies were called the Base Force. The most detailed explanation of this new strategy was found in the unclassified version of the 1992 Joint Military Net Assessment (JMNA) released by the Joint Chiefs of Staff in August 1992.[12] As of early 1996 a new, complete JMNA had not been declassified.[13]

The 1992 JMNA identified the primary new threat to the United States as "instability and being unprepared to handle a crisis or war that no one predicted or expected." The growing complexity of the world's security environment made "it increasingly difficult to predict the circumstances under which US military power might be employed." The United States would continue to retain forward-based forces to deter traditional threats, such as North Korea, but "new planning will be focused primarily on regional contingencies where specific threats are unknown and uncertain."

As defined by the JMNA, key national security objectives were:

- Deter any aggression that could threaten the security of the United States and its allies and -- should deterrence fail -- repel or defeat military attack and end the conflict on terms favorable to the United States, its interests, and its allies.
- Effectively counter threats to the security of the United States and its citizens and interests short of armed conflict, including the threat of international terrorism.

- Preclude any hostile power from dominating a region critical to our interests, and strengthening the barriers against the reemergence of a global threat to those interests.
- Improve stability by pursuing equitable and verifiable arms control agreements, modernizing our strategic deterrent, developing systems capable of defending against limited ballistic missile strikes, and enhancing appropriate conventional capabilities.
- Foster restraint in global military spending and discourage military adventurism.
- Prevent the transfer of militarily critical technologies and resources to hostile countries or groups, especially the spread of chemical, biological, and nuclear weapons and associated high-technology means of delivery.
- Reduce the flow of illegal drugs into the United States by encouraging reduction in foreign production, combating international traffickers, and reducing demand at home.
- Ensure access to foreign markets, energy, mineral resources, the oceans, and space.
- Strengthen and enlarge the commonwealth of free nations that share a commitment to democracy and individual rights.
- Strengthen international institutions like the United Nations to make them more effective in promoting peace, world order, and political, economic, and social progress.
- Maintain stable regional military balances to deter those powers that might seek regional dominance.
- Aid in combating threats to democratic institutions from aggression, coercion, insurgencies, subversion, terrorism, and illicit drug trafficking.

According to the 1992 JMNA, "Deterrence remains the primary and central motivating purpose underlying our national military strategy." U.S. strategy also "presumes that America will provide the leadership needed to promote global peace and security. It will do so by building on the depth we gained for our strategic position with the end of the Cold War and by using our positive influence and leadership to shape the future security environment....Improvements in East-West relations have shifted our focus away from the threat of global war to regional threats of consequence to US vital interests." The JMNA noted that although the United States would "emphasize multinational operations under the auspices of international bodies such as the United Nations," U.S. forces "must be able to act unilaterally when and where US interests dictate."

JMNA observed that the new regional strategy of the United States was "more complex than the containment strategy of the Cold War era." The new strategy was based on four foundations:

1. *Strategic deterrence and defense.* The "maintenance of a modern, fully capable, and reliable strategic deterrent remains the number one defense priority of the United States."

2. *Forward presence.* "For the past 45 years, the day-to-day presence of US forces in regions vital to US national interests has been key to averting crises and preventing war....Although the numbers of US forces stationed overseas will be reduced, the credibility of our capability and intent to respond to crises will continue to depend on judicious forward presence."

3. *Crisis response.* "Regional contingencies we might face are many and varied and could arise on very short notice. US forces must be able to respond rapidly to deter and, if necessary, fight unilaterally or as part of a combined effort....Our strategy also recognizes that when the United States is responding to one substantial regional crisis, potential aggressors in other areas may be tempted to take advantage of our preoccupation."

4. *Reconstitution.* "As military forces are reduced in response to the demise of the global threat, we must preserve a credible capability to forestall a hostile, nondemocratic power from competing militarily with the United States. This reconstitution capability is intended to deter such a power from militarizing and, if deterrence fails, to provide us an expanding warfighting capability necessary to defend our interests."

Building upon these foundations, JMNA identified the strategic principles comprising the national military strategy of the United States. These principles included:

- *Readiness.* "Deterrence and crisis response dictate that we maintain a force that can respond quickly, prepared to fight upon arrival."
- *Collective security.* "We expect to strengthen world response to crises through multilateral operations under the auspices of international security organizations" such as the U.N., formal alliances such as NATO, *ad hoc* coalitions where no formal security relationships exist, and bilateral relationships. The United States must "also retain the capability to operate independently, as our interests dictate."
- *Arms control.* Useful "not as a end in itself but as a means to enhance our national security," arms control bounds "uncertainty" and reduces "nuclear, chemical, biological, and conventional arsenals in many meaningful and lasting ways."
- *Maritime and aerospace superiority.* "Achieving and maintaining preeminence in the air, in space, and at sea is key to our continued success as a global leader. In peace, maritime and aerospace superiority

enhance our deterrent capabilities. In war, they are critical to the conduct and successful termination of conflict."

- *Strategic agility.* The need to respond to regional crises on short notice requires that American forces have the ability to assemble quickly where they are needed from where they are located.
- *Power projection.* "Our ability to project power, both from CONUS [continental United States] and from forward-deployed locations, has strategic value beyond crisis response [including] deterrence, regional stability, and collective security. It becomes an even more critical part of our military strategy because overseas presence will be reduced and our regional focus has been enhanced."
- *Technological superiority.* The United States must rely heavily on qualitative advantages "to offset quantitative advantages [of other countries], minimize risk to US forces, and enhance the potential for swift, decisive termination of conflict."
- *Decisive force.* "One of the essential elements of our strategy is the ability to rapidly assemble the forces needed...to overwhelm our adversaries and thereby terminate conflicts swiftly with minimum loss of life."

Even though the United States must "retain the potential to defeat a global threat should one emerge...our plans and resources are primarily focused on deterring and fighting regional rather than global wars." Forward presence and crisis response were fundamental to the regionally oriented strategy. JMNA explained:

> In peacetime, our forward presence is the "glue" that helps hold alliances together, builds cooperative institutions, and helps countries work together -- including some countries with historical antagonisms. Forward presence helps to reduce regional tensions, deter potential aggressors, and dampen regional arms competition. On a day-to-day basis, our forward presence is an effective vehicle for shaping the future security environment. It is universally recognized as a means of communicating our values and interests and displaying our commitment to peaceful conduct among nations. It is a tangible representation of our global leadership and, as such, it is of immeasurable help in preserving our strategic depth at comparatively low cost....Our forward presence is also the leading edge of our crisis-response capability.

JMNA stated that crisis response "gives us the ability to project force and decisively use military force as determined by the national leadership. Potential threats remain -- countries with substantial or growing military capability -- that, coupled with a trigger such as an age-old antagonism, could erupt into crisis....We do not know whether one of today's potential threats will become the next crisis or if some new threat will evolve to create a crisis in the coming years. Thus, we are focusing our planning efforts on regions of potential conflict. We must be able to project power to Europe, the Middle East, and Asia rapidly and in sufficient strength to defeat any aggressor not deterred by our demonstrated resolve and forward presence."

JMNA stated, "The magnitude and duration of forward-presence operations in a particular region are a function of the importance of US interests and the nature of the threats to those interests. As US interests and the threats to those interests change, our forward-presence operations are adjusted." However, in the post-Cold War period, "fewer forces will be committed to fixed forward-presence roles."

The new U.S. military strategy of regional contingencies emphasized preplanned options for a wide range of crises. These plans "encompass all the instruments of national power (diplomatic, political, economic, and military) to clearly demonstrate US resolve, deter potential adversaries, and, if necessary, deploy and employ forces to fight and win quickly and decisively." JMNA said:

> The precise nature of a US response to a crisis will be predicated on the criticality of US interests at stake, our commitments to the nations involved, the level and sophistication of the threat, and the capabilities of US and allied forces. Before committing US forces to combat, it must be determined that US vital interests are at risk and that political, diplomatic, and economic measures have failed to correct the situation or have been ruled out for some other reason. Our strategy is to resolve swiftly and decisively any conflict in which we become involved, in concert with our allies and friends.

The forces needed to execute the regional contingency strategy were called the Base Force. According to the 1992 JMNA, the Base Force would be comprised of the following toward the end of the decade:

- *Strategic Forces.* B-52H, B-1B, B-2 bombers; 550 missiles; 18 nuclear ballistic missile submarines
- *Army.* 12 active divisions; 6 reserve divisions; 2 cadre divisions
- *Navy.* 450 ships, including 12 aircraft carrier battle groups; 11 active air wings; 2 reserve air wings
- *Marine Corps.* 2.5 active Marine Expeditionary Forces; 1 reserve division and wing

- *Air Force*. 15.25 active fighter wing equivalents (FWEs); 11.25 reserve FWEs.

The Base Force would be organized into four military force packages and four supporting capabilities. The force packages included strategic forces, Atlantic forces, Pacific forces, and contingency forces. The supporting capabilities included transportation, space, reconstitution, and research and development.

The 1992 JMNA noted that with the fall of the Soviet Union, "the massive military threat to Western Europe has virtually disappeared." Henceforth, "Planning will be focused primarily on regional contingencies -- anticipating the conditions under which crises might arise, constructing response plans, and equipping flexible forces to deal with them." The most important common factors in these future crises were:

1. "A US response may be unilateral or multilateral, as a member of a formal alliance or a member of a multinational, *ad hoc* coalition."
2. "The precise location and nature of the crisis that will call for a US military response is unpredictable."
3. "US military actions will be part of a coordinated economic, diplomatic, and public affairs response."
4. "US military responses will employ a `decisive force' designed to be powerful enough to overwhelm the enemy's forces and achieve US objectives with low risk and minimal casualties."
5. "The US Armed Forces will be expected to conduct humanitarian assistance, disaster relief, and peacekeeping operations."

To plan for the type and level of forces needed to respond effectively to regional contingencies, JMNA used a scenario-based analysis that was representative of the existing security environment. It was assumed that an initial, defensive response would be made to the crisis and then a larger, decisive force would be deployed for a counteroffensive to achieve victory. For planning purposes, the assumptions also included a second major crisis occurring simultaneously threatening U.S. interests elsewhere in the world. The 1992 JMNA studied two such scenarios: a surprise North Korean attack against South Korea and an aggressor threatening U.S. interests in Southwest Asia.

According to JMNA, in both scenarios there were adequate forces available to the United States to respond successfully to the first crises. Reaction to second crises was also possible but presented major difficulties. "The Base Force is capable of resolving quickly -- with low risk -- only one major regional crisis at a time. For two crises occurring close together, the United States would have to employ economy of force and sequential operations and make strategic choices. The risk to US objectives in either case is no more than moderate, but there is little margin for unfavorable circumstances."

In making its final assessment, JMNA said: "The end of the Cold War signals a dramatic improvement in the prospects for peace, but the world remains dangerous and turbulent....Throughout the world, instability may lead to a crisis at almost any moment -- requiring the United States to commit its Armed Forces to protect its vital interests and meet alliance commitments, rescue non-combatants, suppress insurgencies and insurrections, or restore lawful governments and territory....The prospect of a large-scale European or global war is more remote now than at any time since 1945. For the near- and mid-term, threats to our interests are much more likely to arise from regional conflicts, instability, terrorism, or drug-trafficking."

JMNA warned that while trends in the international environment generally were favorable for the United States, U.S. forces were "approaching the point where, if capability is reduced further, the United States will have to alter its position of leadership in the world and redefine its objectives and policies."

Policies Toward Asia

The strategy of regional contingencies was a major accomplishment of the Bush administration. Another strategic success was the defining of a coherent post-containment strategy toward Asia, major portions of which were adopted by the Clinton administration in its strategy to build a "new Pacific community." Bush's strategy, which was generally referred to as the East Asian strategic initiative process, was characterized by two elements: a traditional concern with maintaining a favorable balance of power in the region, and a new concern with advancing -- particularly in the economic sphere -- greater regional integration into a community of market democracies. Several major themes were involved. First, the United States would remain committed to the Asian Pacific region, despite reductions of forward based forces due to the end of the Cold War. Second, the United States would continue to focus on bilateral relations with Asian countries with only limited attention paid to multilateral regional relations. Third, U.S. policy would be characterized as "integration in economics" and "diversity in defense."[14] And fourth, the unique U.S. role in Asia would be defined in terms of sustaining the "dynamic balance" of the region.[15]

President Bush outlined his major foreign policy goals toward Asia in a speech to the Asia Society in New York in November 1991.[16] He said the United States was deeply committed to the Asian Pacific, a region of overwhelming economic importance. Asia had the world's fastest growing rate of economic expansion, was the largest trading partner of the United States, and together with the United States generated half of the world's GNP. In the post-Cold War period, Bush said, the United States will remain large and powerful in the Pacific, but it wanted to deepen relationships with Asian nations on the basis of true partnership to build foundations of democracy and freedom. He said three central issues in U.S.-Asian relations were of paramount concern to the United States: security, democracy, and trade. As its long-term goal, the United States sought to build "a commonwealth of freedom."

Details of the Bush administration's policies toward Asia were presented by Secretary of State Baker in Tokyo at the same time as the president's speech in New York.[17] The secretary said: "This is the heart of my message to you: America's destiny lies across the Pacific as well as the Atlantic. The development of an enduring sense of community in this diverse and dynamic region is fundamental to the new international system we are shaping together. And we will only be successful in building this system through a full partnership between Japan and the United States." Baker said the overall structure of U.S. engagement in the Pacific could be envisioned as a

> fan spread wide, with its base in North America and radiating westward. Its central support is the alliance and partnership between the United States and Japan. To the north, one spoke represents our alliance with the Republic of Korea. To the south, another line extends to our ASEAN colleagues. Further south, a spoke reaches to Australia....Connecting these spokes is the fabric of shared economic interests now given form by the Asia-Pacific Economic Cooperation (APEC) process. Within this flexible construct, new political and economic ties offer additional support for cooperative actions by groups of Pacific nations. Over time, we should strive to draw China and the Soviet Union or the Russian republic closer to this system....The flexibility of this structure suits the vast geographic expanse, diversity, and multiple security concerns of East Asia and the Pacific.

Baker emphasized the importance of U.S. bilateral security relations in the region. "In the future, our bilateral security ties will continue to provide geopolitical balance, enable us to serve as an honest broker, and reassure against uncertainty. But multilateral actions may also supplement these bilateral ties." The secretary cautioned against expecting too much from multilateral efforts: "At this stage in this new post-Cold War era, we should be attentive to the possibilities for such multilateral action without locking ourselves into an overly structured approach. Form should follow function."

Noting that economic dynamism was the major distinguishing quality of East Asia, Baker said that growing "intra-Asian and trans-Pacific trade and investment provide the broad common interests on which to build the Pacific community." According to the secretary, the Asia-Pacific Economic Cooperation (APEC) process was "as much a hallmark of our engagement in the region as are our security ties." Baker expressed the hope that, over time, APEC could overcome its "structural inefficiencies through coordinated efforts" and become an important part of economic growth in the region, contributing to trade liberalization and support for an open global trading regime.

Baker said the proposed North American Free Trade Agreement (NAFTA) between the United States, Canada, and Mexico would not establish common trade barriers to those outside. "It would not be in the United States' own interests to isolate ourselves within one economic region of the world. Our future depends on strong economic ties with all regions, as well as a successful GATT system."

Baker observed that the enduring sense of community which the United States wished to build in Asia not only had economic and security elements, but also a foundation of common values. "Without such a foundation, alliances and other ties will not have resilience, since relations based solely on realpolitik can fracture as circumstances change." Baker said these common values included universal concerns for human dignity, individual welfare, and freedom of thought and expression. He emphasized the need for continued progress in democracy and human rights, and called on other nations to work with the United States for "the promotion of political as well as economic reform in the few remaining Marxist-Leninist states in Asia."

Regarding the future, Baker said, "America's fate is ever more closely tied to East Asia and the Pacific....[our] security is inextricably linked to stability in Asia." The secretary promised, "While we will make adjustments in our military posture to fit changing circumstances, we intend to firmly maintain our alliance relationships and our forward-deployed forces." He said, "Our interest in the security and stability of Asia is overriding; our commitment is unshakable; our engagement is beyond question."

The Balance Wheel of Asia

One key strategic concept of the Bush administration was the role of the United States as the balance wheel of Asia. The concept became the catch-phrase to describe U.S. strategy in the Asian Pacific region, replacing containment as the primary justification for continued forward deployed U.S. military forces.

In a statement before the House Foreign Affairs subcommittee on Asia and the Pacific in February 1990, Assistant Secretary of State for East Asian and Pacific Affairs Richard Solomon stressed the strategic necessity for the United States to sustain the balance of power in Asia.[18] In the context of the U.S. goal to create "a new partnership in the Pacific," the United States should play a role "as the dynamic balancer in Asia...crucial to regional -- and global -- stability in the 1990s."

Solomon said the remolding of the security consensus in the East Asia and Pacific region was a high priority for the Bush administration. He noted, "For four decades, the United States has been the central unifying hub of a network of bilateral security relationships in the Pacific. We are the dynamic balancer, the buffer force, and the ultimate security guarantor in a region of great political, cultural, and historical diversity."

A new strategic environment was unfolding in Asia with the emergence of new power centers in Japan, China, and India. At the same time, the region had the world's largest armies standing in an uneasy coexistence. Solomon warned, "Any diminishing of the credibility of the U.S. forward deployed deterrent would only produce an increase in regional tensions, with other powers tempted to fill any perceived gaps. For the foreseeable future, we -- and most nations in the region -- view the United States as the irreplaceable balancing wheel. No other power is viewed as an acceptable substitute for our critical stabilizing role."

The role of the United States as the balance wheel of Asia was explained in a Defense Department report to the Congress entitled *A Strategic Framework for the Asian Pacific Rim: Looking Toward the 21st Century.*[19]

East Asia Strategic Initiative

The *Strategic Framework* report was submitted in April 1990 by the Office for International Security Affairs (ISA). This first East Asia Strategic Initiative (EASI-I) document said the United States needed to redefine its strategy in Asia in the post-Cold War era. The study argued that, in spite of the reduced Soviet threat, U.S. interests in the Asian Pacific would remain similar to those of the past. Those interests were identified as being:

- protecting the United States from attack
- supporting U.S. global deterrence policy
- preserving U.S. political and economic access to the region
- maintaining the balance of power to prevent the rise of any regional hegemony
- strengthening the Western orientation of Asian nations
- fostering the growth of democracy and human rights
- deterring nuclear proliferation
- ensuring freedom of navigation.

Similarly, the basic elements of U.S. Asian strategy would continue to remain valid. According to the report, "forward deployed forces, overseas bases, and bilateral security arrangements [remain] essential to maintaining regional stability, deterring aggression, and preserving U.S. interests."

Because of these continuities with the past, the Pentagon concluded that the existing U.S. military presence should remain largely intact. Some reductions (mostly in ground forces) should take place, however, to reflect the improved international climate and to help reduce the U.S. budget deficit.

According to the report, U.S. military adjustments would occur in three phases. In Phase I (1990-1993) an initial reduction of 14,000-15,000 personnel out of some 135,000 U.S. troops forward deployed in the Pacific would take place. Some 7,000 personnel would be removed from Korea (5,000 Army and 2,000 Air Force); between 5,000 and 6,000 Air Force and Army personnel would be withdrawn from Japan; and approximately 2,000 personnel would be transferred from the Philippines.

Phase II (1993-1995) and Phase III (1995-2000) adjustments would depend on the international situation prevailing at the time. The United States would have a sustainable presence in the region by the end of Phase III. The study said U.S. forward deployed forces in Japan would remain over the long-term with few changes. U.S. air forces would remain at Misawa, for example, and an aircraft carrier task force would remain homeported at Yokosuka. Facilities on Okinawa would also be retained. U.S. forces in Korea would be the minimum necessary to maintain deterrence, with Republic of Korea forces taking a leading role in Korean defense.[20]

Defense Department officials described the future role of the U.S. military in the Western Pacific as a "regional balancer, honest broker, and ultimate security guarantor."[21] Another phrase used to describe the role of the U.S. military was an "irreplaceable balance wheel." Other officials said the mission of the U.S. military was a "central stabilizing role." Richard Solomon used the term "arbiter" to describe the U.S. role.[22]

By thus defining the U.S. role, the Bush administration changed U.S. strategy in the Asian Pacific region from containment to a more traditional emphasis on maintaining a regional balance of power. The *Strategic Framework* study noted that one of the enduring U.S. interests in Asia was "maintaining the balance of power to prevent the rise of any regional hegemony." The report said the U.S. presence "has contributed to regional peace, stability, and prosperity by providing the balance necessary to ensure that no single state assumed a hegemonic position."[23]

Under the new plan, the United States would preserve the balance of power in Asia by: (a) maintaining a strong forward deployed military force in the region for the purposes of deterrence and, if need be, early military response to a crisis; (b) coordinating policies with other Asian Pacific nations through bilateral and multilateral channels to minimize conflict and to maximize regional stability and prosperity; and (c) playing the role of "honest broker" to help resolve problems between the Asian nations themselves.

The *Strategic Framework* report justified the retention of the U.S. force posture in Asia at approximately the same levels maintained during the Cold War on the grounds that: (a) Russia continued to maintain very credible forces in Northeast Asia; (b) such a forward based U.S. posture was necessary because of the proliferation of advanced weapons among regional powers; and (c) sophisticated U.S. systems, including aircraft carrier battle groups, had to be available in case of crises on the Korean peninsula or elsewhere in the region.

In February 1991 the Department of Defense sent a follow-up report to the Congress stating that the *Strategic Framework* study had been well-received by Asian nations and was being implemented according to schedule.[24] In mid-1992 the Pentagon submitted a second progress report on its strategy toward the Asia-Pacific region.[25] The EASI-II (East Asia Strategy Initiative - II) report outlined U.S. security strategy toward the Asian Pacific region through 1995 and took into consideration the demise of the Soviet Union and the Philippines' decision to end U.S. bases on its territory. In February 1995 a third EASI report was submitted to Congress by the Clinton administration, a document summarized in Chapter 3.

EASI-II observed that with the collapse of the Soviet Union and the end of the Cold War, U.S. regional roles in Asia, "which had been secondary in our strategic calculus, have now assumed primary importance in our security engagement in the Pacific theater." The report emphasized the continued importance of U.S. forward presence in Asia, a military presence that "has underpinned stability in East Asia and helped secure its economic dynamism" and "has made the US the key regional balancer, contributed to regional stability, enhanced US diplomatic influence, and contributed to an environment conducive to the growth of US economic interests." The report said, "Maintaining a credible security presence is an important element in our effort to build a sense of Asia-Pacific community vital to the post-Cold War international system now taking place."

EASI-II redefined somewhat the U.S. security interests in Asia, the fundamental security missions of U.S. military forces in the region, and basic principles of U.S. policy toward Asia. Enduring U.S. security interests in Asia were said to be: protecting the United States and its allies from attack; maintaining regional peace and stability; preserving U.S. political and economic access; contributing to nuclear deterrence; fostering the growth of democracy and human rights; stopping proliferation of nuclear, chemical and biological weapons, and ballistic missile systems; ensuring freedom of navigation; and reducing illicit drug trafficking.

The fundamental security missions of U.S. forces in the Pacific were listed as: defending Alaska, Hawaii, and the connecting lines of communication (LOCs) to the continental United States; protecting U.S. territories and Freely Associated States for which the United States has defense responsibilities; assisting U.S. allies in their defense; and maintaining the security of the LOCs throughout the Pacific as well as the Persian Gulf, Indian Ocean, and the East and South China Seas.

EASI-II said U.S. security policy toward Asia was guided by six basic principles:

- assurance of American engagement in Asia and the Pacific
- a strong system of bilateral security arrangements
- maintenance of modest but capable forward-deployed U.S. forces
- sufficient overseas base structure to support those forces
- assumption of greater responsibility of U.S. allies for their own defense
- complementary defense cooperation.

EASI-II did not specify existing threats to U.S. interests in Asia, but rather noted potential sources of instability that the United States had to be prepared to meet. These included:

- North Korea, particularly its "quest for a nuclear weapons capability" and "uncertainties surrounding the pending political transition"
- communist states of Asia, which "will change, but it is difficult to predict whether the process will proceed peacefully or violently"
- the PRC, where "politics will almost certainly be volatile as Deng Xiaoping and the current octogenarian leaders pass from the scene"
- Taiwan, whose future relationship with mainland China was uncertain
- Cambodia, which still confronted the terrorism of the Khmer Rouge
- the Philippines, threatened by terrorism and insurgency from the communist New People's Army
- Spratly Islands, whose territory and waters were claimed by China, Taiwan, Vietnam, the Philippines, Malaysia, and Brunei
- Burma, under a military dictatorship which refused to recognize the results of the 1990 elections and tended to ignore narcotics activities within its borders
- proliferation, particularly missile exports from North Korea and China and the nuclear weapons program of Pyongyang.

With the loss of its Philippine bases in 1991-1992, EASI-II said the United States would shift its force posture in Southeast Asia from having a large permanent presence in the region to one of having a forward presence accommodated by access agreements with countries such as Singapore and Australia. "Through wider regional access in Southeast Asia, we intend to promote our continued, stabilizing presence in the region into the next century."

The report emphasized the strategic importance of U.S. forces based in Japan. The U.S. force posture in that country would remain at high levels, with strong naval, air, and ground force deployments. Japan would continue "to be America's key Pacific ally and the cornerstone of US forward deployed defense strategy in the Asia-Pacific region. The Japanese archipelago affords US forward deployed forces geostrategically crucial naval, air and ground bases on the periphery of the Asian land mass....our presence in Japan remains a vital aspect of our forward deployed posture. US military forces based in Japan contribute to the security of Japan and are well located for rapid deployment to virtually any trouble spot in the region." The presence of U.S. forces in Japan were considered permanent, although some adjustments would be possible as Japan assumed greater responsibility for defense of the home islands and sea lane defense out to 1,000 nautical miles.

U.S. forward deployed forces in Korea were primarily intended to deter a North Korean attack. The level of forces were more flexible, being determined by variables such as the extent of the North Korean threat and the ability of the Republic of Korea (ROK) to defend itself. "Over the long-term, US forward peacetime presence will be reduced somewhat, while sustaining the ability to reinforce the ROK in wartime....We envision a US presence in the ROK as long as the Korean people and government want us to stay and threats to peace and stability remain."

Overall, changes in U.S. deployments through 1995 were to be minor. EASI-II summarized these as follows:

- In Japan, U.S. forces in 1990 were 50,000; these were reduced to 45,227 by the end of 1992 and would reach 44,527 in 1995. The major reductions occurred at the end of 1992 when 3,489 Marines were transferred out of Okinawa.
- In Korea, U.S. forces in 1990 were 44,400; these were reduced to 37,413 by the end of 1992. A further reduction to 30,913 by 1995 was put on hold because of the North Korean nuclear weapons program. Most of these reductions occurred in U.S. Army personnel (5,000 withdrawn by the end of 1992) and Air Force personnel (1,987 withdrawn by the end of 1992).
- In the Philippines, all 14,800 personnel in 1990 were withdrawn by the end of 1992. Approximately 1,000 of these were sent elsewhere in the Asian Pacific.
- In addition, there were approximately 25,800 U.S. military personnel "afloat or otherwise forward deployed." This figure would remain constant from 1990 through 1995.

In total, the United States had 135,000 military personnel in the Asian Pacific region in 1990. By the end of 1992 these had been reduced to 109,440. EASI-II projected that by the end of 1995 total U.S. troop levels in Asia would be 102,240 (assuming the phased reduction of some 6,500 troops from Korea proceeded according to schedule). Of the

109,440 U.S. military personnel in the region at the end of 1992, 45,227 were in Japan (2,000 Army; 6,500 shore-based Navy; 21,500 Marines; 15,400 Air Force); 37,413 were in South Korea (27,000 Army; 400 shore-based Navy; 500 Marines; 9,500 Air Force); 1,000 troops were being redeployed in the region from the Philippines; and 25,800 were "afloat or otherwise forward deployed."

EASI-II was released at approximately the same time as the 1992 Joint Military Net Assessment document discussed earlier. JMNA's comments on the role of the Asian Pacific region in the new U.S. strategy of regional contingencies deserve mention. According to JMNA, "US interests in the Pacific, including Southeast Asia and the Indian Ocean, require a continuing commitment." U.S. forward presence operations in the Pacific furthered three fundamental purposes of the national security strategy: (1) "deterring threats to US interests by providing tangible evidence of our commitment"; (2) "providing for regional stability and improving our initial crisis response capability by maintaining forces in forward locations, establishing lines of communication and access agreements, and familiarizing forces with the regions in which they may have to fight"; and (3) "enhancing US influence by lending credibility to our alliances and friendships with other countries." JMNA went on to explain:

> The presence of US forces serves as a stabilizing influence in this economically important area. Geography, US interests, and the nature of potential threats dictate the need for joint forces similar to but smaller than those present today. Forward-presence forces will be principally maritime, with half our projected carrier and amphibious force oriented toward this area, including one forward-deployed CVBG [aircraft carrier battle group] and one MEF [Marine Expeditionary Force]. We plan to keep one CVBG and one ARG [amphibious readiness group] homeported in Japan and have developed new forward-basing options not dependent on our former bases in the Republic of the Philippines. The improving military capability of South Korea has enabled our Army forces to be trimmed to less than a division. Air forces can be reduced to two or three FWEs [Fighter Wing Equivalents] in Korea and Japan. The pace of the reductions is gauged to shifting to a supporting role in Korea and modulated by North Korea's actions and nuclear cooperation. In addition, we retain forces in both Alaska and Hawaii.

JMNA noted that U.S. "forces oriented toward the Pacific must be sufficient to demonstrate that the United States will continue to be a prominent military power and remain vitally interested in the region." The North Korean threat remained the primary concern of U.S. forces, requiring American troops on the peninsula and reinforcement capabilities. "As South Korea continues to improve its military capabilities, we expect to be able to reduce our ground and air presence." U.S. crisis response forces focused on the Pacific region were stationed in Hawaii, Alaska, and the continental United States. These included one reinforced Army division, one Fighter Wing Equivalent, and five aircraft carrier battle groups.

Thus, according to security plans formulated by the Bush administration at the close of the Cold War, by 1995 and through the remainder of the century, half of the U.S. aircraft carrier battle groups and underway replenishment groups would be assigned to the Pacific, as well as two-thirds of the U.S. amphibious ready groups. This substantial military presence -- essentially the same as that maintained during the Cold War -- reflected a continuing U.S. commitment to Asia based on growing American interests in the region. Under President Bush there was little concern in Asia or in the United States about the U.S. commitment to the region or Washington's determination to continue to play a leading role in regional affairs.

Conclusion

The euphoria that greeted the end of the Cold War prompted the Bush administration to look for a new strategy "beyond containment" and to seek a "new world order" in which American ideals of freedom, democracy, justice, and rule by law would prevail in the international system. The vision was attractive to many, but it soon became apparent that the American people were in no mood to finance its implementation. Moreover, many other countries, including China, opposed the U.S. vision of a new world order from the beginning.

The Bush administration tried to define a more realistic view of U.S. global commitments. It developed a strategy of collective engagement to enlarge the community of market democracies through closer cooperation with U.S. friends and allies. The regional contingencies strategy and the Base Force rationalized the process of reducing American military forces while preserving those forces believed necessary to protect American interests. In Asia this meant the retention of much of the existing force structure, with some reduction of personnel. Under the East Asian strategic initiative, U.S. strategy and policy toward the Asian Pacific changed very little with the end of the Cold War, although the U.S. role was recast as an essential balancing wheel to ensure regional stability. Virtually all of these strategic themes were reintroduced -- after minor repackaging -- by the Clinton administration.

In the case of China, the Bush administration found itself in a quandary. It wanted to cooperate with the PRC on issues important to U.S. interests. However, after Tiananmen Beijing's domestic and foreign policies, as well as the opinion of the American people and the Congress, made friendly Sino-American relations impossible. During the Bush administration, U.S. relations with China were severely strained on fundamental issues such as trade, missile and nuclear proliferation, human rights, the new international order, and the respective roles of China and the United States in Asia. Through persistent efforts, Bush was able to secure several important agreements in the areas of trade and proliferation with Beijing toward the end of his term. These agreements enabled Sino-American relations to continue without complete reversal, and they provided a foundation on which incoming President Bill Clinton could build his own Asian and China policies.

Notes

1. For the major phases of U.S. involvement with Asia and the enduring qualities that characterize Asian-American relations, see Akira Iriye, "The American Experience in East Asia," in Mary Brown Bullock and Robert S. Litwak, eds., *The United States and the Pacific Basin: Changing Economic and Security Relationships* (Washington, D.C.: Woodrow Wilson Center Press, 1991), pp. 13-29.

2. See William T. Tow, *Encountering the Dominant Player: U.S. Extended Deterrence Strategy in the Asia-Pacific* (New York: Columbia University Press, 1991).

3. Ibid., p. 410. In this statement, Tow paraphrases George Kennan.

4. George Bush, "Security Strategy for the 1990s," *Department of State Current Policy*, No. 1178 (May 1989).

5. Bush made the comment in an address to a Joint Session of Congress. See *New York Times*, September 12, 1990, p. A20.

6. This international backing gave the United States the political, moral, and allied military (including host nation) support necessary to prosecute a successful war in the difficult political environment of the Middle East.

7. While the United States made up 70 percent of the armed forces fighting the Iraqis, other nations -- principally Saudi Arabia, Kuwait, Japan, and Germany

-- financed most of its expenses. According to the Office of Management and Budget, the total cost of the Persian Gulf War to the United States was $61 billion. Pledges from coalition partners were about $54 billion, of which $48.2 billion was in cash and $5.4 billion was in kind, mostly fuel. *New York Times*, August 16, 1991, p. D2.

8. George Bush, "Address by the President on the State of the Union" (Washington, D.C.: The White House, Office of the Press Secretary, January 29, 1991).

9. *Washington Post*, March 7, 1991, p. A32.

10. George Bush, "Address by the President to the Air University" (Washington, D.C.: The White House, Office of the Press Secretary, April 13, 1991).

11. James A. Baker III, "A Summons to Leadership," *Dispatch* (Washington, D.C.: Department of State Bureau of Public Affairs, 1992).

12. *1992 Joint Military Net Assessment* (Washington, D.C.: Joint Chiefs of Staff, August 1992).

13. The Joint Chiefs of Staff did release a 1993 declassified version of JMNA, but this was a highly truncated document stating that, pending completion of the Clinton administration's Bottom-up Review of Strategy and Force Structure, the "abbreviated 1993 JMNA serves as a bridge from the 1992 to the 1994 JMNA." In November 1995 the author was told by Pentagon officials that the 1994 JMNA would not been made public.

14. Richard H. Solomon, "Asian Security in the 1990s: Integration in Economics, Diversity in Defense," *Department of State Dispatch*, Vol. 1, No. 10 (November 5, 1990). Solomon was Assistant Secretary of State for East Asian and Pacific Affairs.

15. Richard H. Solomon, "Sustaining the Dynamic Balance in East Asia and the Pacific," *Department of State Current Policy*, No. 1255 (February 1990).

16. George Bush, "Remarks by the President to the Asia Society" (Washington, D.C.: The White House, Office of the Press Secretary, November 12, 1991).

17. James A. Baker III, "The U.S. and Japan: Global Partners in a Pacific Community" (Tokyo: U.S. Department of State, Office of the Assistant Secretary/Spokesman, November 11, 1991).

18. Richard H. Solomon, "Sustaining the Dynamic Balance in East Asia and the Pacific."

19. *A Strategic Framework for the Asian Pacific Rim: Looking Toward the 21st Century* (Washington, D.C.: Office of the Assistant Secretary of Defense for International Security Affairs, April 1990). The report was a requirement contained in the FY 1990 Defense Authorization Act. Henceforth referred to as *A Strategic Framework*.

20. The U.S. presence in the Philippines became untenable when the Philippine Senate refused to ratify a new U.S.-Philippine Treaty of Friendship, Cooperation, and Security signed in August 1991.

21. See "Statement of Paul Wolfowitz, Under Secretary of Defense for Policy before the Senate Armed Services Committee," April 19, 1990, pp. 8-9, ms.

22. Richard H. Solomon, "Asian Security in the 1990s: Integration in Economics, Diversity in Defense."

23. *A Strategic Framework*, pp. 2, 5.

24. *A Strategic Framework for the Asian Pacific Rim: Looking Toward the 21st Century: A Report to Congress* (Washington, D.C.: Department of Defense, February 28, 1991).

25. *A Strategic Framework for the Asian Pacific Rim: Report to Congress 1992* (Washington, D.C.: Department of Defense, 1992).

2

Principles of Clinton's Foreign Policy

In December 1992 President-elect Bill Clinton described his foreign policy strategy as one of "American engagement" in the world. Indeed, "engagement" became one of the administration's key terms to define its strategy to preserve U.S. leadership in the post-Cold War period. Clinton's strategy of engagement pursued three main objectives:

1. the restructuring of U.S. military forces to reduce the cost of defense to the American people
2. cooperation with U.S. allies to encourage the spread and consolidation of democracy and free markets worldwide
3. reestablishment of American economic leadership to stimulate global growth and prosperity.[1]

These objectives were encapsulated by Secretary of State-designate Warren Christopher during his confirmation hearings before the Senate Foreign Relations Committee in January 1993. He said the Clinton administration would base its foreign policy on the "three pillars" of economic growth, military strength, and support for democracy.[2]

Christopher explained the "three pillars" in a speech to the Chicago Council on Foreign Relations in March 1993.[3] Reflecting the priority placed on economic matters by the Clinton administration, Christopher said foreign policy should first and foremost serve the economic needs of the United States. The U.S. government should ensure that foreign markets are open to American goods, services, and investments, and it should press other wealthy nations to do their part to stimulate global economic growth. Second, the armed forces of the United States should be "more agile, mobile, flexible and smart," even while they are being reduced and their budgets shrunk. Third, democracy and respect for human rights should be encouraged abroad since "history has shown that a world of more democracies is a safer world, is a world that will devote more to human development and less to human destruction."

The "three pillars" of economic growth, a strong but smaller U.S. military, and the encouragement of democracy and human rights abroad remained the strategic objectives of the Clinton administration through 1995. There was nothing remarkable about these objectives -- most administrations in the twentieth century had pursued similar goals -- but their prioritization was an issue. During the forty years of the Cold War, the United States had placed priority on security due to the communist threat. By the time Clinton became president in 1993, however, that global threat had disappeared. In its place were a number of potential regional threats that did not threaten the survival of the United States but rather various important interests. Thus, while maintaining a strong military force remained an objective of the Clinton administration, it was no longer considered the highest priority.

In place of defense, Clinton stressed national economic growth. Many of his political supporters, however, wanted to raise the importance of expanding democracy and protecting human rights. Both economic prosperity -- which required trade -- and the promotion of democracy and human rights abroad necessitated U.S. involvement overseas. And American leadership overseas required a strong, forward deployed military force. Thus, although the Clinton administration clearly preferred to deal with domestic issues, from the outset it had to focus as well on foreign affairs and national security. Because of the close connection between economic growth, security, and encouragement of democracy, the administration sought to do all three simultaneously without establishing definitive priorities.

The inability to prioritize made articulation of a practical national security strategy difficult. The Clinton administration wanted to retain U.S. leadership in the world, but it also wanted to reduce defense and foreign affairs expenditures. How to maintain U.S. influence over global affairs while shrinking resources committed to that purpose became a central strategic dilemma for President Clinton.

This dilemma became apparent early in the administration. In May 1993 a top State Department official told reporters that the Clinton administration would focus primarily on domestic economic issues. Since the United States had only limited resources, it must "define the extent of its commitment commensurate with those realities. This may on occasion fall short of what some Americans would like and others would hope for." To compensate for its reduced unilateral role in world affairs, the administration would work much more closely with its allies in collective security endeavors to protect U.S. interests.[4]

Concerned over the negative impression that the administration was retreating from global leadership, Secretary Christopher emphasized America's leadership role in a speech at the University of Minnesota a few days later. "The need for American leadership is undiminished. The United States stands prepared to act decisively to protect our interests wherever and whenever necessary. When it is necessary, we will act unilaterally....Where collective responses are more appropriate, we will lead in mobilizing responses....But make no mistake: we will lead."[5]

Assertive Multilateralism

One of the first efforts by the Clinton administration to define a new foreign policy strategy came in the form of "assertive multilateralism." U.S. Ambassador to the United Nations Madeleine K. Albright told the Senate in early June 1993 that the administration's approach to Somalia and other difficult Third World crises was an assertive multilateralism. She explained, "There will be many occasions when we need to bring pressure to bear on the belligerents of the post-Cold War period and use our influence to prevent ethnic and other regional conflicts from erupting. But usually we will not want to act alone -- our stake will be limited and direct U.S. intervention unwise."[6]

Assertive multilateralism implied U.S. leadership working through multilateral channels such as the United Nations to achieve American foreign policy goals and objectives. The types of U.N. action the Clinton administration said it would support included humanitarian relief in the case of civil strife or natural disasters, countering threats to democratically elected governments, containing situations where a local conflict might spread to a regional conflagration, and deterring threats to international security.

Presidential Decision Directive 13 (PDD-13), signed by President Clinton in August 1993, put the assertive multilateralism strategy into effect. The directive committed the United States to support U.N. peacemaking and peacekeeping operations, as well as to help the U.N.

expand its headquarters staff to better handle international emergencies. The directive rejected U.S. support for a U.N. rapid deployment force, but it did earmark U.S. assets to assist U.N. operations on a case-by-case basis. American commanders serving under U.N. command in these operations were instructed to disobey U.N. orders if they were illegal or "militarily imprudent."[7]

Public support for assertive multilateralism quickly waned as the practical limitations of this approach were demonstrated in Bosnia and Somalia, where the United States experienced great frustration in attempting to support U.N. peacekeeping operations. The failure of assertive multilateralism forced the administration to define more carefully its foreign policy and national security strategies, although strong elements of multilateralism were retained -- as seen in U.S. participation in NATO's occupation of Bosnia in late 1995.

Strategy of Enlargement

In September 1993 national security advisor Anthony Lake announced at John Hopkins University that the United States would adopt a new strategy of "enlargement" to replace the Cold War strategy of containment.[8] "Enlargement," combined with Clinton's earlier concept of "engagement," became the U.S. national security strategy through the end of 1995.

Lake said U.S. engagement in international affairs throughout the twentieth century "was animated both by calculations of power and by this belief: to the extent democracy and market economics hold sway in other nations, our own nation will be more secure, prosperous and influential, while the broader world will be more humane and peaceful." The essence of U.S. foreign policy was that "we must promote democracy and market economics in the world -- because it protects our interests and security; and because it reflects values that are both American and universal."

During the Cold War the United States "contained a global threat to market democracies." Now, Lake explained, "the successor to a doctrine of containment must be a strategy of enlargement -- enlargement of the world's free community of market democracies." There were four components of this new strategy.

First, "we should strengthen the community of major market democracies -- including our own -- which constitutes the core from which enlargement is proceeding." In this, "renewal starts at home," since Americans must be strong domestically before they have the will or capacity to engage in commitments abroad. In addition, it was vitally important that the United States renew "the bonds among our key democratic allies," especially Europe, Canada, and Japan. Relations with each of these allies were "basically sound," but they suffered from an "economic problem and a military problem."

The economic problem was "shared sluggish growth and the political cost it exacts on democratic governments." Lake warned: "Unless the major market democracies act together -- updating international economic institutions, coordinating macroeconomic policies and striking hard but fair bargains on the ground rules of open trade -- the fierce competition of the new global economy, coupled with the end of our common purpose from the Cold War, could drive us into prolonged stagnation or even economic disaster." The military problem centered on finding a new role for NATO in the post-Cold War era. "We will seek to update NATO, so that there continues behind the enlargement of market democracies an essential collective security."

The second imperative of the strategy of enlargement, Lake explained, "must be to help democracy and markets expand and survive in other places where we have the strongest security concerns and where we can make the greatest difference." He assured his audience: "This is not a democratic crusade; it is a pragmatic commitment to see freedom take hold where that will help us most." In terms of priorities, "we must target our effort to assist states that affect our strategic interests, such as those with large economies, critical locations, nuclear weapons or the potential to generate refugee flows into our own nation or into key friends and allies." Further, "We must focus our efforts where we have the most leverage. And our efforts must be demand-driven -- they must focus on nations whose people are pushing for reform or have already secured it." Lake said "pursuing enlargement in the Asian Pacific" was of strategic importance to the United States.

The third element of the strategy of enlargement," Lake said, "should be to minimize the ability of states outside the circle of democracies and markets to threaten it." Observing that "democracy and market economics have always been subversive ideas to those who rule without consent," Lake cautioned, "we should expect the advance of democracy and markets to trigger forceful reactions from those whose power is not popularly derived."

In these cases of "backlash states," U.S. policy "must seek to isolate them diplomatically, militarily, economically and technologically....When the actions of such states directly threaten our people, our forces, or our vital interests, we clearly must be prepared to strike back decisively and unilaterally....We must always maintain the military power necessary to deter, or if necessary defeat, aggression by these regimes. Because the source of such threats will be diverse and unpredictable, we must seek to ensure that our forces are increasingly ready, mobile, flexible and smart."

Lake said, "We cannot impose democracy on regimes that appear to be opting for liberalization, but we may be able to help steer some of them down that path, while providing penalties that raise the costs of repression and aggressive behavior." As an example, Lake pointed to China:

> These efforts have special meaning for our relations with China. That relationship is one of the most important in the world, for China will increasingly be a major world power, and along with our ties to Japan and Korea, our relationship with China will strongly shape both our security and economic interests in Asia. It is in the interest of both our nations for China to continue its economic liberalization while respecting the human rights of its people and international norms regarding weapons sales....We seek a stronger relationship with China that reflects both our values and our interests.

The fourth component of the U.S. strategy of enlargement, Lake said, "involves our humanitarian goals, which play an important supporting role in our efforts to expand democracy and markets." Public pressure may drive U.S. humanitarian engagement, but other more pragmatic factors must be considered as well: "cost; feasibility; the permanence of the improvement our assistance will bring; the willingness of regional and international bodies to do their part; and the likelihood that our actions will generate broader security benefits for the people and the region in question." These practical considerations "suggest there will be relatively few intra-national ethnic conflicts that justify our military intervention."

As for multilateralism, "only one overriding factor can determine whether the US should act multilaterally or unilaterally, and that is America's interests. We should act multilaterally where doing so advances our interests -- and we should act unilaterally when that will serve our purpose. The simple question in each instance is this: what works best?"

A few days after Lake's speech, President Clinton discussed his foreign policy in a speech to the United Nations General Assembly.[9] The president said there were two great forces in the world influencing international relations: integration and disintegration. Making clear that he stood on the side of integration, he said the United States intended to "remain engaged and to lead," and while "we cannot solve every problem...we must and will serve as a fulcrum for change and a pivot point for peace."

Clinton described his strategy of enlargement in this way: "Our overriding purpose must be to expand and strengthen the world's community of market-based democracies. During the Cold War we sought to contain a threat to survival of free institutions. Now we seek to enlarge the circle of nations that live under those free institutions." He noted that "nonproliferation, conflict resolution, and sustainable development" were the principal security challenges to the democratic community he was seeking to enlarge.

The administration thus defined its national security strategy in terms of engagement and enlargement during its first year in office. It was apparent, however, that President Clinton focused more on domestic issues than international relations. He told the *Washington Post* in October 1993, "it's simply not possible for the United States to become the ultimate resolver of every problem in the world." Although the United States must remain engaged in the world for its own security, economic, and humanitarian interests, "we've simply got to focus on rebuilding America." He said the American people voted for him instead of George Bush because they wanted the president to concentrate on domestic issues in the post-Cold War era.[10]

Clinton's assessment of American preferences was probably accurate; foreign affairs was a low priority in the absence of a major threat to U.S. security. When asked about their major concerns, only 3 percent of those polled by the *Washington Post* in January 1994 listed foreign policy as the area in which Clinton should work hardest to solve. Listed above foreign policy were, in order of priority: dealing with violent crime, reforming the nation's health care system, creating jobs, strengthening the nation's economy, dealing with the illegal drug problem, reducing the federal budget deficit, and reforming the welfare system. The only public policy issue ranked less important than handling foreign affairs was bringing needed change to government.[11]

Engagement and Enlargement

The Clinton administration formally defined its national security strategy of "engagement and enlargement" in two, almost identical statements released by the White House in July 1994 and February 1995.[12] The statements were very similar to the remarks of national security advisor Anthony Lake in his September 1993 speech at John Hopkins University.

In his preface to the national security strategy statements, President Clinton described engagement and enlargement as "a new national security strategy for this new era." The central goals of the strategy were "to sustain our security with military forces that are ready to fight," "to bolster America's economic revitalization," and "to promote democracy abroad."

The president emphasized that "the line between our domestic and foreign policies has increasingly disappeared...we must revitalize our economy if we are to sustain our military forces, foreign initiatives and global influence, [and] we must engage actively abroad if we are to open foreign markets and create jobs for our people."

> We believe that our goals of enhancing our security, bolstering our economic prosperity, and promoting democracy are mutually supportive. Secure nations are more likely to support free trade and maintain democratic structures. Nations with growing economies and strong trade ties are more likely to feel secure and to work toward freedom. And democratic states are less likely to threaten our interests and more likely to cooperate with the U.S. to meet security threats and promote sustainable development.

Reflecting both "America's interests and our values," the president said the strategy was "based on enlarging the community of market democracies while deterring and containing a range of threats to our nation, our allies and our interests." The strategy had three "central components": (1) efforts to enhance U.S. security by maintaining a strong defense capability and promoting cooperative security measures; (2) efforts to open foreign markets and spur global economic growth; and (3) efforts to promote democracy abroad.

The documents said it was essential for the United States to continue to exercise world leadership. "In this time of global change, it is clear we cannot police the world; but it is equally clear we must exercise global leadership. As the world's premier economic and military power, the U.S. is indispensable to the forging of stable political relations and open trade." When possible, the United States "must stress preventive diplomacy" to resolve problems before they become crises. U.S. engagement also must be selective, "focussing on the challenges that are most relevant to our own interests and focussing our resources where we can make the most difference."

U.S. efforts abroad could be unilateral, in alliance and partnership, or multilateral, depending upon what best served U.S. interests. The United States must be "willing to act unilaterally when our direct national interests are most at stake; in alliance and partnership when our interests are shared by others; and multilaterally when our interests are more general and the problems are best addressed by the international community."

The importance of coalition strategy was emphasized. "The threats and challenges we face demand cooperative, multinational solutions. Therefore, the only responsible U.S. strategy is one that seeks to ensure U.S. influence over and participation in collective decisionmaking in a wide and growing range of circumstances....Accordingly, a central thrust of our strategy of engagement is to sustain and adapt the security relationships we have with key nations around the world."

Maintaining a strong conventional defense capability was crucial to U.S. security in the post-Cold War era. The strategy of engagement and enlargement required "robust and flexible military forces" to accomplish a variety of tasks, including: to deter and, if necessary, defeat adversaries in two nearly simultaneous major regional crises in locations such as North Korea and Iran or Iraq; to provide a credible overseas presence through robust overseas deployments; to combat the spread and use of weapons of mass destruction and their advanced means of delivery such as missiles; to contribute to multilateral peacekeeping, peace enforcement, and other operations in conjunction with the United Nations; and to support counterterrorism, anti-drug trafficking, and other missions.

The national security strategy defined guidelines on how and when U.S. military forces would be employed overseas, noting that "our national interests will dictate the pace and extent of our engagement." In cases involving the survival of the United States or its vital interests, "our use of force will be decisive and, if necessary unilateral." In cases where a threat exists to important but not vital U.S. interests, "military forces should only be used if they advance U.S. interests, they are likely to be able to accomplish their objectives, the costs and risks of their employment are commensurate with the interests at stake, and other means have been tried and have failed to achieve our objectives. Such uses of force should also be limited, reflecting the relative saliency of the interests we have at stake."

In cases involving humanitarian interests, U.S. non-combat military resources would be used, although combat forces may be deployed temporarily to stabilize a situation before turning the operation over to international relief agencies. "As much as possible, we will seek the help of our allies or of relevant multilateral institutions." Also, "our engagement must meet reasonable cost and feasibility thresholds" so that U.S. military action will likely bring lasting improvement.

In addition to conventional military forces, other critical elements enhancing U.S. security were nonproliferation and counterproliferation efforts, sufficient nuclear forces "to deter any future hostile foreign leadership with access to strategic nuclear forces from acting against our vital interests," arms control efforts, peace operations with the United Nations, and intelligence properly directed in the post-Cold War international environment.

Clinton's national security strategy also stressed the promotion of prosperity at home and democracy abroad as central strategic objectives. The primary economic goal was "to strengthen the American economy and reverse the decline in American competition." Key programs included enhancing U.S. access to foreign markets through the North American Free Trade Agreement (NAFTA), the Asia Pacific Economic Cooperation (APEC) process, the completion of the Uruguay Round of GATT and establishment of the new World Trade Organization, the U.S.-Japan Framework for Economic Partnership Agreement, and the Summit of the Americas commitment to negotiate a free trade agreement in the Western Hemisphere by 2005. Other programs included strengthening macroeconomic coordination among the major economies, providing for energy security, and promoting sustainable economic development abroad.

In terms of promoting democracy, "All of America's strategic interests -- from promoting prosperity at home to checking global threat abroad before they threaten our territory -- are served by enlarging the community of democratic and free market nations." The United States would work "with new democratic states to help preserve them as democracies committed to free markets and respect for human rights." According to the White House, "The core of our strategy is to help democracy and markets expand and survive in [new places] where we have the strongest security concerns and where we can make the greatest difference. This is not a democratic crusade; it is a pragmatic commitment to see freedom take hold where that will help us most." The

United States would target its efforts "to assist states that affect our strategic interests, such as those with large economies, critical locations, nuclear weapons, or the potential to generate refugee flows into our own nation or into key friends and allies." Moreover, the United States would focus its efforts where it had the most leverage and "on nations whose people are pushing for reform or have already secured it."

Clinton's national security strategy was applied to key regions around the world. East Asia was seen as "a region of growing importance for U.S. security and prosperity." The documents stated: "nowhere are the strands of our three-pronged strategy more intertwined, nor is the need for continued U.S. engagement more evident. Now more than ever, security, open markets and democracy go hand in hand in our approach to this dynamic region." According to the national security statement, "President Clinton envisions an integrated strategy -- a New Pacific Community -- which links security requirements with economic realities and our concern for democracy and human rights." Thus, the creation of a New Pacific Community became, in effect, Clinton's grand strategy for East Asia.

The Bottom-Up Review

President Clinton's strategic concepts and foreign policy principles were translated into defense strategy in a comprehensive "bottom-up" review of U.S. security requirements undertaken by the Pentagon in 1993.[13] The *Report on the Bottom-Up Review*, released to the public in October 1993, said that the most striking change in the U.S. security environment since the end of the Cold War was "in the nature of the danger to our interests." Previously, the greatest danger to the United States was a "global threat from massive Soviet nuclear and conventional forces." Now the threat was more diffuse and included such dangers as:

- the spread of nuclear, biological, and chemical weapons of mass destruction
- aggression by major regional powers or ethnic and religious conflict in regions of strategic importance to the United States
- the potential failure of democratic reform in the former Soviet Union and the reemergence of authoritarian regimes hostile to the United States
- the potential failure to build a strong and growing U.S. economy.

   The report said the United States had an historic opportunity to shape the new world order in ways favorable to American long-term interests. Specifically, the United States could enlarge "the community of nations, guided by a common commitment to democratic principles, free-market economics, and the rule of law." Other opportunities included the expansion of security partnerships with friendly nations, the improvement of regional deterrence, and the protection of U.S. security with fewer resources.

   The U.S. grand strategy resulting from these considerations was "a strategy of engagement, prevention, and partnership." (Elsewhere in the document it was called a "strategy of engagement [with] two characteristics: prevention and partnership.") The report said the United States must pursue a strategy of political, economic, and military engagement in the world to protect and advance its enduring goals. Such a strategy would help achieve two significant results: (1) it would avoid "the risks of global instability and imbalance that could accompany a precipitous U.S. withdrawal from security commitments," and (2) it would help "shape the international environment in ways needed to protect and advance U.S. objectives over the longer term and to prevent threats to our interests from arising." The strategy of engagement

> advocates preventing threats to our interests by promoting democracy, economic growth and free markets, human dignity, and the peaceful resolution of conflict, giving first priority to regions critical to our interests. Our new strategy will also pursue an international partnership for freedom, prosperity, and peace. To succeed, this partnership will require the contributions of our allies and will depend on our ability to establish fair and equitable political, economic, and military relationships with them.

   The report said the "primary task" of the United States in the post-Cold War period was "to strengthen our society and economy for the demanding competitive environment of the 21st century, while at the same time avoiding the risks of precipitous reductions in defense capabilities and the overseas commitments they support."

   To achieve this strategic objective required the United States to build "a coalition of democracies." The report said, "The common values and objectives of democratic nations provide a basis for cooperation across a broad spectrum of policy areas, from deterrence and defense against aggression to the promotion of individual and minority rights." Making the most "of this commonality of values and interests" was in the U.S. strategic interest and required the United States to expand and adapt "mechanisms to facilitate policy coordination and cooperation among democracies."

Sustaining cooperation among allies necessitated "a continued willingness on the part of the United States to act as a security partner and leader...in Europe, East Asia, the Near East, and Southwest Asia." At the same time, ways had to be found "to sustain our leadership at lower cost." The United States had to make clear to its allies "the linkages between a sustained U.S. commitment to their security on the one hand, and their actions in such areas as trade policy, technology transfer, and participation in multinational security operations on the other."

Another key aspect of the U.S. coalition strategy was to encourage "the spread of democratic values and institutions" into new areas. The study mentioned the former Soviet empire as presenting "an unparalleled opportunity" to bring its people into the community of democracies.

The defense strategy arising from these considerations was defined in terms of appropriate U.S. responses to the major "dangers" of the post-Cold War era: the proliferation of weapons of mass destruction, regional threats of various kinds, threats to newly democratic states, and threats to the American economy. Of these threats, the first two were of specific concern to the Department of Defense.

According to the Pentagon report, "The acquisition of nuclear weapons by a regional aggressor would pose very serious challenges" to the United States. North Korea, Iraq, and Iran were specifically mentioned as examples of potentially hostile nations pursuing nuclear weapons programs. These countries possessed other weapons of mass destruction (WMD), such as chemical and biological weapons, and their means of delivery.

U.S. strategy to meet this threat involved several dimensions. Nonproliferation efforts were designed to prevent the spread of WMD through diplomatic means such as "strengthening the provisions of and widening participation in the Nuclear Nonproliferation Treaty, implementing the Chemical Weapons Convention and the Missile Technology Control Regime, and negotiating nuclear testing limitations." U.S. WMD strategy also required "the capability for nuclear retaliation against those who might contemplate the use of weapons of mass destruction" and the improvement of ways "to counter proliferation, such as active and passive defenses against nuclear, biological, and chemical weapons and their delivery systems." The strategy also relied upon counterproliferation capabilities, primarily military means "to deter, prevent, or defend against the use of WMD if our nonproliferation efforts fail."

The second category of threats to U.S. interests in the new era arose from various regional dangers. These included "large-scale aggression; smaller conflicts; internal strife caused by ethnic, tribal, or religious animosities; state-sponsored terrorism; subversion of friendly governments; insurgencies; and drug trafficking." Each of these threatened, "to varying degrees, interests important to the United States." Specific regional dangers included the possibility of war on the Korean peninsula, efforts by Iraq or Iran to dominate the Persian Gulf region, the continuing civil war in Croatia and Bosnia, struggles in central or eastern Europe, state-sponsored terrorism executed in the United States, and drug trafficking in Latin America.

> To address the new regional dangers and seize new opportunities, we have developed a multifaceted strategy based on defeating aggressors in major regional conflicts, maintaining overseas presence to deter conflicts and provide regional stability, and conducting smaller-scale intervention operations, such as peace enforcement, peacekeeping, humanitarian assistance, and disaster relief to further U.S. interests and objectives.

U.S. forces had to be capable of winning two nearly simultaneous regional conflicts. The report explained, "Regional aggressors represent a danger that must be deterred and, if necessary, defeated by the military capability of the United States and its allies. Moreover, if we were to be drawn into a war in response to the armed aggression of one hostile nation, another could well be tempted to attack its neighbor....Therefore, it is prudent for the United States to maintain sufficient military power to be able to win two major regional conflicts that occur nearly simultaneously." An additional benefit was that "sizing our forces for two major regional conflicts provides a hedge against the possibility that a future adversary might one day confront us with a larger-than-expected threat."

U.S. military forces deployed overseas in peacetime played several essential roles in the regional contingencies strategy. These roles included:

- "The peacetime overseas presence of our forces is the single most visible demonstration of our commitment to defend U.S. and allied interests in Europe, Asia, and elsewhere around the world."

- "The presence of U.S. forces deters adventurism and coercion by potentially hostile states, reassures friends, enhances regional stability, and underwrites our larger strategy of international engagement, prevention, and partnership."
- It gives the United States "a stronger influence, both political and economic as well as military, in the affairs of key regions."
- It improves the U.S. "ability to respond effectively to crises or aggression when they occur" and "provides the leading edge of the rapid response capability that we would need in a crisis."
- It enables the United States and its allies to improve their operational cooperation.
- It "helps to ensure our access to the facilities and bases we would need during a conflict or contingency."

The overseas military presence of the United States could take several forms: permanent or long-term stationing of U.S. forces, periodic deployments to crises or joint training exercises, and prepositioning of military equipment to facilitate a rapid buildup in time of crisis. Generally, "Army and Air Force units are permanently stationed in regions where the United States has important and enduring interests and wants to make clear that aggression will be met by a U.S. military response." U.S. maritime overseas forces provide the operational mobility and capability "to bring military power quickly to bear anywhere in the world."

The report noted that U.S. forces would "likely be involved in operations short of declared or intense warfare." Peacekeeping, peace enforcement, and other intervention operations would sometimes be undertaken unilaterally but most often would be part of an international effort. "In deciding where, when, and how our military should be employed" in these types of missions, certain questions need to be answered: Does participation advance U.S. national interests? Are the objectives clear and attainable? How will the intervention affect other U.S. defense obligations? Can the United States contribute capabilities and assets necessary for the success of the mission?

Dangers to democracy and dangers to the economy were two other types of potential threats to U.S. interests. Although they were of less direct concern to the U.S. military, the Department of Defense would assist in both areas. In the case of dangers to democracy, U.S. armed forces would work closely with central and eastern Europe and the former Soviet republics to "help these countries institute democratic, civilian control over the military," help secure and reduce the nuclear weapons held by these countries, and cooperate in multilateral peacekeeping operations. This "defense by other means" would be backed by more traditional methods. "As a hedge against possible reversals, we should strengthen our bilateral and multilateral ties in central and eastern Europe. We must also retain the means to rebuild a larger force structure, should one be needed in the future to confront an emergent authoritarian and imperialistic Russia reasserting its full military potential."

In terms of dangers to U.S. economic interests, military strength would ensure that the United States would have a "seat at the table" in political and economic decisionmaking. Trade and security, the report said, were mutually supportive. Likewise, "military power supports and is supported by political and economic power."

The Bottom-Up Review listed the major objectives for U.S. armed forces in each of the four areas of threat to U.S. interests in the post-Cold War era. To meet the threat from weapons of mass destruction, U.S. military objectives were to deter the use of nuclear, biological, or chemical weapons against the United States, its forces, and its allies; halt or slow the proliferation of WMD; develop capabilities to locate and destroy WMD storage, production, and deployment facilities of potential aggressors; defend U.S. forward deployed forces from WMD; reduce the nuclear arsenals of the former Soviet Union and the United States to lower the threat of nuclear war; and minimize the exposure and vulnerability of U.S. forces to WMD.

To counter the threat of regional dangers, U.S. military objectives were to deter and, if necessary, defeat major aggression in regions important to the United States; be capable of fighting and winning two major regional conflicts nearly simultaneously; prepare U.S. forces to participate effectively in multilateral peace enforcement and unilateral intervention operations; and adapt existing alliances and build new ones to enhance regional and global security.

To meet the threat to democratic reform, U.S. military objectives were to use military-to-military contacts to help foster democratic values in other countries; and protect fledgling democracies from subversion and external threats.

To meet the threat to economic prosperity, U.S. military objectives were to redirect resources to investments that improve both the U.S. defense posture and its competitive position economically; facilitate reinvestment that allows defense industries to shift to nondefense production; support the development of dual-use technologies and encourage the freer flow of technology between the military and civilian sectors; use long-standing U.S. security relationships with key allies and partners to expand economic cooperation and to sustain and enhance global free trade; and actively assist nations in making the transition from controlled to market economies.

The review made important decisions regarding the size of U.S. armed forces necessary to implement the grand strategy of engagement. The most important determining factor was how to win two nearly simultaneous major regional conflicts in areas such as the Korean peninsula and the Persian Gulf. The study said: "During the Cold War, U.S. military planning was dominated by the need to confront numerically superior Soviet forces in Europe, the Far East, and Southwest Asia. Now, the focus is on the need to project power into regions important to U.S. interests and to defeat potentially hostile regional powers, such as North Korea or Iraq. Although these nations are unlikely to threaten the United States directly, they and other countries like them have shown that they are willing and able to field forces sufficient to threaten important U.S. interests, friends, and allies."

Using the scenarios of a North Korean attack against South Korea and a remilitarized Iraqi attack against Kuwait and Saudi Arabia, the report said the Joint Chiefs of Staff envisioned four stages of U.S. combat operations. In phase one, the highest priority "will most often be to minimize the territory and critical facilities that an invader can capture." In phase two, "once an enemy attack has been stopped and the front stabilized, U.S. and allied efforts would focus on continuing to build up combat forces and logistics support in the theater while reducing the enemy's capacity to fight." In phase three, "U.S. and allied forces would seek to mount a large-scale, air-land counteroffensive to defeat the enemy decisively." In the final phase, some U.S. forces would remain "to ensure that the conditions that resulted in conflict did not recur."

The forces needed for successful combat operations in these stages were assessed, along with support requirements in areas such as airlift, prepositioning, sealift, battlefield surveillance, advanced munitions, and aerial refueling. The process determined a building block of forces required to win a single major regional conflict. These combat forces included: four to five Army divisions; four to five Marine Expeditionary Brigades; ten Air Force fighter wings; 100 Air Force heavy bombers; four to five Navy aircraft carrier battle groups; and special operation forces.

Another determinant in sizing U.S. armed forces through the year 2000 was the need to maintain an overseas presence in Europe, Northeast Asia, Southwest Asia, Africa, and Latin America, as well as a global naval presence. The most important ground-based presence would remain in Europe and Northeast Asia. In Europe the United States would retain about 100,000 troops, mostly comprised of substantial elements of two Army divisions and two and one-third wings of Air Force fighters. U.S. naval ships and submarines would continue to patrol the Mediterranean Sea and other waters around Europe.

In Northeast Asia the United States would also retain about 100,000 troops. Troop levels in South Korea would be frozen due to the continuing threat from North Korea. U.S. forces deployed in the Republic of Korea would include one Army division (comprised of two brigades) and one wing of Air Force fighters. On Okinawa the United States would continue to station a Marine Expeditionary Force and an Army special forces battalion. In Japan the United States would homeport the aircraft carrier *Independence*, the amphibious assault ship *Belleau Wood*, and their support ships. One and one-half wings of Air Force fighters would be stationed in Japan and Okinawa, and the U.S. Seventh Fleet would routinely patrol the western Pacific.

In terms of its global naval presence, the United States had in recent years "sought to deploy a sizable U.S. naval presence -- generally, a carrier battle group accompanied by an amphibious ready group -- more or less continuously in the waters off Southwest Asia, Northeast Asia, and Europe." Because of the downsizing of the navy, however, "we will experience some gaps in carrier presence in these areas in the future." In place of carrier battle groups, the United States would sometimes "show the flag" with other major warships such as large-deck amphibious assault ships and Aegis guided-missile cruisers with their accompanying escort vessels.

Weighing these factors, the Bottom-Up Review recommended an overall U.S. force structure to be in place by the year 1999. These forces included:

- Army
  - 10 divisions (active)
  - 5+ divisions (reserve)
- Navy
  - 11 aircraft carriers (active)
  - 1 aircraft carrier (reserve/training)
  - 45-55 attack submarines
  - 346 ships
- Air Force
  - 13 fighter wings (active)
  - 7 fighter wings (reserve)
  - up to 184 bombers (B-52H, B-1, B-2)

- Marines
  - 3 Marine Expeditionary Forces
  - 174,000 personnel (active)
  - 42,000 personnel (reserve)
- Strategic
  - 18 ballistic missile submarines
  Nuclear
  - up to 94 B-52H bombers
  Forces
  - 20 B-1 bombers
  (by 2003)
  - 500 Minuteman III ICBMs (single warhead).

The proposed forces provided a "peace dividend" with a projected savings of about \$91 billion through fiscal year 1999 from the Bush administration's defense program.

Certain changes in the focus of the armed forces would be required. The Army would have to increase its battlefield mobility and flexibility; the Navy would be less focused on sea control and would have to improve its ability to bring power to bear in a land war; and the Air Force would have to concentrate on bringing firepower to regional battlefields.

The report stated that the recommended force structure would enable the United States "to carry forward with confidence our strategy of being able to fight and win two major regional conflicts nearly simultaneously." It would not, however, provide adequate forces to maintain overseas presence and to conduct peacekeeping operations during a period of fighting two major regional conflicts. Moreover, the key to the "force's ability to carry out its strategy are a series of critical force enhancements" in areas such as "additional prepositioning of brigade sets of equipment, increased stocks of antiarmor precision-guided munitions, more early-arriving naval air power, and other initiatives."

Conclusion

President Clinton's strategy of engagement and enlargement was based on certain key assumptions. It was believed that a democratic world would be a safer world for the United States; that democratic nations would cooperate more and fight less than authoritarian states; and that a common system of values would be stronger in international politics than competing national interests.

It was assumed that most potentially hostile nations -- those still under authoritarian rule -- could be changed into regimes more compatible with U.S. interests through peaceful interaction with the West. It was assumed that people were essentially the same everywhere; and that the yearning for a better lifestyle, participation in government decisions, and respect for human dignity were so compelling both in moral and practical terms that change would be forthcoming, if given a chance. It was expected that this change would come through peaceful means in most instances, although hardliners in some countries would pose a militant threat as they sought to preserve their privileges and defend their ideology.

It was strongly believed that America had time on its side in the historic confrontation between democratic and authoritarian systems. The United States had to remain strong to defend the process of democratic expansion and to protect those countries that were vulnerable to authoritarian neighbors. Washington had to continue to exercise global leadership to provide both the stimulus and the direction for positive change. The United States was seen as the essential stabilizing force in world politics because of its unique superpower status and absence of hegemonic ambitions.

The U.S. leadership role had emerged as a result of victories in two world wars and in the Cold War. A continuation of that role was necessary for an orderly transition to a new international system characterized by a cooperative community of market democracies. Since the new order would reflect American values and contain institutions in which the United States exercised great influence, a strategy advancing the new world order was seen as a cost-effective way both to serve U.S. interests and promote U.S. values.

The strategy of engagement and enlargement was designed by the Clinton administration to realize this world view. Clinton intended to preserve the preeminence of the United States as a global power, albeit with fewer resources and lower cost. Moreover, the military power of the United States and its diplomacy were deliberately intertwined with an assertive economic policy and persistent efforts to expand American values.

All of these strands of American foreign policy -- military, diplomatic, economic, and ideological -- were integrated into the strategy of engagement and enlargement. Basic U.S. objectives, interests, and instruments of national power remained consistent with those of the past. President Clinton's major contribution to U.S. strategy in the post-Cold War period was to bring a more integrated and balanced approach to U.S. foreign policy and national security.

Despite the intellectual soundness of this approach, Bill Clinton remained focus primarily on domestic issues. This resulted -- in Asia as elsewhere -- in impressions that the United States was reducing the level of its leadership role in world affairs. Commitments and resources had been brought more into alignment with the strategy of engagement and enlargement, but no strategy could substitute for effective personal leadership from the White House.

The next chapter will examine how Clinton's principles of foreign policy and national security strategy were applied to the Asia-Pacific region. The region was of great interest to the Clinton administration because of its vast opportunities and serious challenges. In East Asia the strategy of engagement and enlargement was reflected in Clinton's vision of a New Pacific Community.

Notes

1. Clinton's foreign policy strategy was summarized by Senator Alan Cranston in his keynote speech before the Sixteenth Joint Conference of the ROC-USA and USA-ROC Economic Councils, Taipei, Taiwan, December 1992, ms.

2. *Washington Post*, January 14, 1993, p. A12.

3. *Washington Post*, March 23, 1993, p. A1.

4. As quoted in *Washington Post*, May 26, 1993, p. A1.

5. *Washington Post*, May 28, 1993, p. A34.

6. *Washington Post*, June 13, 1993, p. A33.

7. For a discussion of PDD-13, see *Washington Post*, August 5, 1993, p. A1. For background to the document, see *Washington Post*, June 18, 1993, p. A1.

8. Anthony Lake, "From Containment to Enlargement," speech delivered to the John Hopkins University School of Advanced International Studies, Washington, D.C., September 21, 1993, ms.

9. "Address by the President to the 48th Session of the United Nations General Assembly" (New York: The White House, Office of the Press Secretary, September 27, 1993).

10. Excerpts from the interview can be found in *Washington Post*, October 17, 1993, p. A28.

11. The results of the poll, conducted nationwide with interviews with 1,005 adults between January 14-18, 1994, were summarized in *Washington Post*, January 23, 1994, p. A9.

12. *A National Security Strategy of Engagement and Enlargement* (Washington, D.C.: The White House, July 1994); ibid., February 1995.

13. Les Aspin, *Report on the Bottom-Up Review* (Washington, D.C.: Department of Defense, October 1993). In most areas of strategy and policy, the review was similar to the 1992 JMNA discussed in the previous chapter.

3

The New Pacific Community

The first major statement of Clinton foreign policy toward Asia was given in March 1993 by Winston Lord, former U.S. Ambassador to China, who was appointed Assistant Secretary of State for East Asian and Pacific Affairs.[1] Lord told the Senate Foreign Relations Committee that the Clinton administration would seek to build a "new Pacific community" with ten goals to guide U.S. policy:

1. Forging a revitalized global partnership with Japan that reflected a more mature balance of responsibilities.
2. Erasing the nuclear threat and moving toward peaceful reconciliation on the Korean peninsula.
3. Restoring firm foundations for cooperation with China while pursuing greater political openness and economic reform.
4. Deepening ties with the Association of Southeast Asian Nations (ASEAN) as it broadens its membership and scope.
5. Obtaining the fullest possible accounting of U.S. missing in action as Washington moves to normalize relations with Vietnam.
6. Securing a peaceful, independent, and democratic Cambodia.
7. Strengthening the Asia Pacific Economic Cooperation (APEC) process as the cornerstone of economic cooperation in the Pacific.
8. Developing multilateral forums for security consultations while maintaining U.S. alliances.
9. Spurring regional cooperation on global challenges like the environment, refugees, health, narcotics, nonproliferation, and arms sales.
10. Promoting democracy and human rights.

Lord said, "In the aftermath of the Cold War, economics is increasingly supplanting military considerations on our foreign policy agenda. More than ever our national security depends on our economic strength. With domestic renewal now America's highest priority, trade and investment are critical. And no region is more central for American economic interests than the world's most dynamic one -- Asia." Lord noted that the Asia-Pacific region was the world's largest consumer market and the biggest export market for the United States. In 1992 Asia bought $128 billion worth of American products while Europe purchased $111 billion. U.S. exports to Asia provided more than two million American jobs.

Lord said U.S. policy would "confront our Asian economic challenges and opportunities on several levels." First, "foreign policy begins at home -- strengthening our competitiveness is a *sine qua non* for an effective policy." Second, "the successful completion of the Uruguay Round [of GATT] is the most urgent multilateral task." Third, "bilaterally we must continue to pry open Asian markets, particularly in those nations running large surpluses with us" such as Japan and China. In addition, "greater regional cooperation is required." The most promising vehicle in this regard was the Asia Pacific Economic Cooperation (APEC) forum, whose members comprised half of the world's GNP in 1992.[2]

In the area of security, Lord said, "By virtue of history and geography the United States is the one major power in Asia not viewed as a threat. Virtually every country wants us to maintain our security presence. While balance-of-power considerations have declined in the wake of the Cold War, they remain relevant as Asian-Pacific nations contemplate their fates. Each ones harbors apprehensions about one or more of its neighbors. A precipitous American military withdrawal would magnify these concerns. Add the increasing resources available for weapons purchases in the rapidly growing Asian nations and there is a recipe for escalating arms races and future confrontations that could threaten U.S. interests."

Lord noted that Clinton security policy toward Asia comprised several dimensions: a "reaffirmation of our treaty alliances with Japan, Korea, Australia, Thailand, and the Philippines"; "military arrangements under the Compact of Free Association" with the Marshall Islands, Micronesia, and Palau; "the maintenance of a substantial military presence" forward deployed in the region; and "prudent modifications" of the U.S. military presence after consultations with its allies. Lord emphasized that U.S.

allies in the region "can and must assume a growing share of the security burden."

A new element in U.S. security policy toward Asia was Clinton's support for multilateral security discussions centered in Southeast and Northeast Asia. Lord said:

We welcome increased security consultations in the framework of the ASEAN Post Ministerial Conference. This process can usefully encourage nations to share information, convey intentions, ease tensions, resolve disputes and foster confidence. The United States will fully participate.

For the first time in this century, there are no adversarial fault lines among the great powers in Northeast Asia: the United States, Japan, Russia and China. The post-Cold War period invites dialogue to prevent arms races, the forging of competing alignments, and efforts by one power or group of powers to dominate this strategic region. Our voice will be crucial. In close concert with our Pacific allies, we could engage Russia, China and others inside and outside Northeast Asia.

The administration did not seek a formal security pact in the region. Lord commented: "Asia is not Europe. We do not envisage a formal CSCE-type [Conference on Security and Cooperation in Europe] structure. But it is time to step up regional discussions on future security issues. We are open-minded on the arenas."

Noting that President Clinton had determined that "promoting democracy must be one of the central pillars of our foreign policy," Lord said the "spread of liberty not only affirms American values but also serves our interests [because] open societies do not attack one another. They make better trading partners. They press for environmental reform. They do not practice terrorism. They do not produce refugees." However, the pursuit of democracy "cannot be our only foreign goal; we must weigh geopolitical, economic and other factors. Nor do we seek to impose an American model; each nation must find its own way in its own cultural and historical contexts. But universal principles of freedom and human rights belong to all, the peoples of Asia no less than others." The administration would "deal pragmatically with authoritarian governments," but at the same time "press universal principles....Whenever possible, we should work with others to expand the frontiers of freedom."

Lord observed that in Asia several global issues were of concern to the United States, including: the proliferation of dangerous weapons in countries such as North Korea, which "now poses the greatest threat to our security"; the world's population growth, with half of the world's population living in Asia and a billion more people to be living there within twenty years; severe environmental problems in Asia, ranging from deforestation, China's burning of coal, and the threat of global warming to Pacific Island states; the potential of major refugee migrations in Asia in the future due to poverty, repression, and uncertain political succession; and the traffic in drugs, especially "the supply of narcotics from Burma and neighboring countries."

Lord also discussed U.S. bilateral relations with key Asian countries such China. In the case of the PRC, the Clinton administration would follow a carefully nuanced policy that would balance the PRC's importance as a major country with its continued abuse of human rights and pursuit of certain policies inimical to U.S. interests. The administration would be guided by the three Sino-American communiqués of 1972, 1979, and 1982; would leave China and Taiwan alone to work out their future relationship, insisting only that the process be peaceful; would not challenge the principle of there being only "one China"; would continue to build unofficial relations with Taiwan based on the 1979 Taiwan Relations Act; and would make clear the U.S. humanitarian and commercial stakes in the future of Hong Kong, scheduled to revert to Chinese sovereignty in 1997.

Hence, from the outset of the Clinton administration there was an effort to bring to Asia the essential elements of engagement and enlargement. U.S. regional strategy centered around the building a new Pacific community with the critical U.S. interests being economic growth, security, and the expansion of democracy. As in the Bush administration, China was seen as a major challenge to U.S. policy, necessitating a nuanced approach that would maintain cooperative relations with Beijing while dissuading its leaders from actions inimical to U.S. interests in areas such as proliferation, trade, and human rights.

Building Blocks of Pacific Community

Reflecting his intention to place high priority on Asia, Clinton's first overseas trip as president was to Japan and Korea in July 1993. After taking part in the Group of Seven (G-7) meeting of the heads of government of the United States, Japan, Canada, Great Britain, France, Germany, and Italy, held in Tokyo that year, Clinton travelled to the Republic of Korea. The president explained his strategy to build the new

Pacific community in speeches at Waseda University in Tokyo on July 7 and the Korean National Assembly in Seoul on July 10.

At Waseda Clinton said the new community would rest upon five building blocks: (1) "a revived partnership between the United States and Japan"; (2) "progress toward more open economies and greater trade"; (3) "support for democracy"; (4) "the firm and continuing commitment of the United States to maintain its treaty alliances"; and (5) the U.S. commitment to maintain "its forward military presence in Japan and Korea and throughout this region."[3]   The president explained the "economic essentials" for the new Pacific community and his support for democracy at Waseda University. He discussed security policy in Seoul.

In his Waseda speech Clinton noted that Asia's imports of $2 trillion were creating "a tripolar world, driven by the Americas, by Europe, and by Asia."   Asia's growing economic strength increased the region's importance to the United States. To build a new Pacific community "our first international economic priority must be to create a new and stronger partnership between the United States and Japan."   Since the two countries produced nearly 40 percent of the world's output and "neither of us could thrive without the other," the U.S. relationship with Japan was "the centerpiece of our policy toward the Pacific community."

Although the security and political aspects of the U.S.-Japan relationship were sound, "our economic relationship is not in balance" due to a persistently high U.S. trade deficit. "It is clear that our markets are more open to your products and your investments than yours are to ours....Our people understand when our nation has a huge trade deficit with an emerging economy like China. The same was true just a few years ago with Korea and Taiwan. But both those nations have moved closer to trade balance with the U.S. as they have become more prosperous. The same has not happened with Japan." The president emphasized: "What the United States seeks is not managed trade or so-called trade by the numbers, but better results from better rules of trade."

A second economic building bloc for the new Pacific community was "a more open regional and global economy."   This meant resistance against protectionist pressures, the successful completion of the Uruguay Round of the GATT negotiations, and the reduction of regional trade barriers. The president said the North American Free Trade Agreement (NAFTA) would not close North America to the rest of the world but open it up. He suggested the possibility of an Asian-Pacific free trade area, remarking that "the most promising economic forum we have for debating a lot of these issues in the new Pacific community is the Organization for Asian-Pacific Economic Cooperation, APEC."

The third priority in building a new Pacific community was "to support the wave of democratic reform sweeping across this region." Economic growth, combined with the information age, had made people's craving for freedom irresistible. "This spread of democracy is one of the best guarantees of regional peace and prosperity and stability that we could ever have in this region." Also, the movement toward democracy was "the best guarantor of human rights." Clinton said:

> It is not Western urging or Western imperialism, but the aspiration of Asian peoples themselves that explain the growing number of democracies and democratic movements in this region....Each of our Pacific nations must pursue progress while maintaining the best of their unique cultures. But there is no cultural justification for torture or tyranny. We refuse to let repression cloak itself in moral relativism. For democracy and human rights are not Occidental yearnings; they are universal yearnings.

In his address to the Korean National Assembly President Clinton outlined the fundamentals of security for the new Pacific community and the role of the United States.[4] He emphasized that, in Asia, "we must always remember that security comes first." He assured his audience that "the United States intends to remain actively engaged in this region. America is, after all, a Pacific nation. We have many peoples from all over Asia now making their home in America....We have fought three wars here in this century. We must not squander that investment." Clinton said, "The best way for us to deter regional aggression, perpetuate the region's robust economic growth, and secure our own maritime and other interests is to be an active presence. We must and we will continue to lead."

The president pointed to four security priorities for the new Pacific community: "First, a continued American military commitment to this region. Second, stronger efforts to combat the proliferation of weapons of mass destruction. Third, new regional dialogues on the full range of our common security challenges. And, last, support for democracy and more open societies throughout this region."

"The bedrock of America's security role in the Asian Pacific," Clinton explained, "must be a continued military presence." He reaffirmed the five U.S. bilateral security agreements with Korea, Japan, Australia, the Philippines, and Thailand. These agreements "enable the U.S. Armed Forces to maintain a substantial forward presence. At the same time they have enabled Asia to focus less energy on an arms race and more energy on the peaceful race toward economic development and opportunity for the peoples of this region."

"The second security priority for our new Pacific community is to combat the spread of weapons of mass destruction and their means of delivery." The most dangerous threat to Asian security was nuclear proliferation, with North Korea's nuclear program pointed to as an example. Clinton cited North Korea's "indiscriminate sales of the SCUD missiles" as another example of the proliferation problem, noting that Pyongyang was developing a longer ranged missile of 600 miles that could threaten Osaka from North Korea or Tel Aviv from Iran. Moreover, the president said, "We have serious concerns...about China's compliance with international standards against missile proliferation."

In terms of the third security priority for the new Pacific community, the president observed: "The challenge for the Asian Pacific in this decade...is to develop multiple new arrangements to meet multiple threats and opportunities. These arrangements can function like overlapping plates of armor individually providing protection and together covering the full body of our common security concerns." Examples of such multiple arrangements included "groups of nations confronting immediate problems" such as North Korea's nuclear program; "peacekeeping" operations such as the U.N.-sponsored mission to Cambodia; and "confidence-building measures to head off regional or subregional disputes."

In addition to these arrangements, the president supported new regional security dialogues. ASEAN's post-ministerial conference and a Northeast Asian security forum were mentioned as examples. Regional economic organizations like APEC could also play a role in easing regional tensions. "The goal of all these efforts," Clinton said, "is to integrate, not isolate, the region's powers." As far as China was concerned, the United States was attempting to convince Beijing to be a responsible member of the international community while at the same time involving China in regional security, political, and economic affairs.

As his fourth security priority, President Clinton emphasized the contributions to peace that democratic progress can make.

Ultimately, the guarantee of our security must rest in the character and the intentions of the region's nations themselves. That is why our final security priority must be to support the spread of democracy throughout the Asian Pacific. Democracies not only are more likely to meet the needs and respect the rights of their people, they also make better neighbors. They do not wage war on each other, practice terrorism, generate refugees or traffic in drugs and outlaw weapons. They make more reliable partners in trade and in the kind of dialogues we announced today.

Secretary of State Warren Christopher reiterated these themes during his visit to Singapore in July 1993 to take part in the annual ASEAN Post-Ministerial Conference. He explained the security, economic, and democratic policies of the new administration to the conference on July 26.[5] The most important security issue in the region was "the need for strong international efforts to combat the spread of weapons of mass destruction and their means of delivery." Christopher said, "First and foremost, the United States is committed to tough and effective global rules to halt the spread of nuclear weapons." In this regard, "North Korea's adherence to the Non-Proliferation Treaty and its full compliance with its IAEA [International Atomic Energy Agency] safeguards obligations and the North-South [Korean] Denuclearization Declaration are essential. The United States is determined to see a non-nuclear Korean peninsula."

The secretary said, "A second major challenge is the proliferation of chemical and biological weapons of mass destruction and the missiles that can deliver them." This was a growing problem for Asia, "because economic and technological development means the region can now produce chemicals, sophisticated electronics, and other products and services that the proliferators want, but are now denied in Europe and the U.S." Christopher emphasized the need for Asian governments to participate in relevant international agreements and export control regimes.

Another security challenge was "the need to respond to conflicts around the globe through collective engagement [in which] the nations of Asia and the Pacific have a vital part to play." Christopher said, "At the regional level, the post Cold-War dynamic has produced radical shifts in old balances of power. A new Pacific community must create a new regional balance that promotes stability, regional arms control and the peaceful resolution of disputes." New regional security dialogues were needed to meet common challenges. However, "we envision not the building of blocs against a common threat but rather intensified discussions among nations which may harbor apprehensions about others' intentions." Christopher explained:

Underlining a change in U.S. policy, President Clinton announced at the Korean National Assembly earlier this month that we will participate actively in regional security dialogues in Asia. We believe such discussions can complement our bilateral relationships, help reduce tensions, enhance openness and transparency and prevent destabilizing arms races. These dialogues should therefore be inclusive: the U.S. welcomes the progressive integration of China and Russia, as well as others, in this ASEAN-PMC framework. As the President said, "These arrangements can function like overlapping plates of armor...covering the full body of our common security concerns." Let me emphasize, however, that regional security dialogues in no way supplant America's alliances or forward military presence in Asia. Rather, they are supplements to ensure a peaceful and stable Asia in the post-Cold War era.

Christopher also stressed the importance of economics to the new Pacific community, pointing to APEC as "the cornerstone of regional economic cooperation" and "a focal point for building a new Pacific community." The secretary emphasized that if the U.S. government was to receive public support for remaining engaged in Asia, "Asia's markets must be open to American goods and services."

As the third element of U.S. policy toward Asia, Christopher reaffirmed U.S. support for democracy and human rights. Since "freedom is linked to development, prosperity, and the spread of market principles," the United States believed the expansion of democracy in Asia was inevitable, as seen in democratic progress in Taiwan, Korea, the Philippines, Thailand, Mongolia, and even Cambodia. Christopher said, "We respect the religious, social, political, and cultural characteristics that make each of our countries unique." At the same time, the United States was "pleased that, despite differing perspectives, all of our countries were able to agree at the World Human Rights Conference in Vienna [June 1993] that human rights are universal. Cultural, social, and other differences cannot justify denying those rights."

Among the many policy issues that confronted the Clinton administration in its efforts to build a new Pacific community, two were of special interest: APEC and North Korea. APEC represented U.S. efforts to push integration forward in the Pacific, whereas the suspected North Korean nuclear weapons program was a pragmatic security concern of first magnitude. These two policy issues serve as examples of how President Clinton sought to implement his strategy in the Asian Pacific in the 1993-1994 period.

Asia-Pacific Economic Cooperation

The most ambitious regional initiative undertaken by the Clinton administration was the invigoration of the Asia-Pacific Economic Cooperation (APEC) forum as an instrument of economic integration and free trade. APEC was established in November 1989 by the governments in the region for the purpose of promoting trade and investment in the Pacific Basin. The United States was chairman of APEC in 1993, hosting its fifth annual ministerial meeting in Seattle, Washington, in November of that year. During the Seattle meeting, Mexico and Papua New Guinea were added to the membership, which comprised Australia, New Zealand, the six ASEAN states, Japan, South Korea, China, Taiwan (designated as Chinese Taipei), Hong Kong, Canada, and the United States.

The Clinton administration placed high priority on APEC because of the economic importance of its members to the U.S. economy. In 1992 the fifteen APEC members had a combined gross regional product of more than $14 trillion, while their share of world trade approached 35 percent, or $2.3 trillion. U.S. exports to other APEC members totalled $219 billion, or 49 percent of total U.S. exports. U.S. imports from other APEC members totalled $313 billion, or 59 percent of U.S. imports. Total U.S. trade with APEC constituted 54 percent of U.S. global trade, compared to 24 percent with Europe and the former Soviet Union.[6]

President Clinton explained his support of APEC in Seattle on November 19, 1993.[7] With the collapse of communism and the Soviet threat, the United States was at a turning point in its history. "More than ever, our security is tied to economics." Specifically, U.S. security "depends upon enlarging the world's community of market democracies because democracies are more peaceful and constructive partners."

To exert leadership in the global economy, the United States had to "pursue a three-part strategy. First, we must continue to make our economy and our people more competitive. Second, we must focus our global initiative on the fastest-growing regions. Third, we must create new arrangements for international relations so the forces of this new era benefit our people as well as our partners."

Clinton recalled, "For decades, our foreign policy focused on containment of communism, a cause led by the United States and our European allies....But as our concern shifts to economic challenges that are genuinely global, we must look across the Pacific as well as the Atlantic." Asia was the largest U.S. trading partner, and "We do not intend to bear the cost of our military presence in Asia and the burdens of regional leadership only to be shut out of the benefits of growth that stability brings....we must use every means available in the Pacific, as elsewhere, to promote a more open world economy through global agreements, regional efforts and negotiations with individual countries."

It was necessary to "develop new institutional arrangements that support our national economic and security interests internationally." This endeavor included "working to build a prosperous and peaceful Asian Pacific region through our work here with APEC." The president said, "The mission of [APEC] is not to create a bureaucracy that can frustrate economic growth, but to help build connections among economies to promote economic growth."

Immediately following the APEC ministerial conference in Seattle, President Clinton hosted the first-ever meeting of Asian-Pacific leaders on nearby Blake Island. No substantive agreements were reached, but the president said APEC leaders found a consensus vision of the Asian-Pacific community: "We've agreed that the Asian Pacific region should be a united one, not divided. We've agreed that our economic policies should be opened, not closed....we're helping the Asian Pacific to become a genuine community; not a formal, legal structure, but rather a community of shared interests, shared goals and shared commitment to mutual beneficial cooperation."[8]

The sixth APEC ministerial meeting convened in Jakarta, Indonesia, in November 1994 to begin to flesh out the consensus vision reached at Blake Island. In attendance were ministers from the previous meeting, plus Chile as a new member. In addition to reconfirming "trade and investment liberalization as a cornerstone of APEC's identity and activity," the ministers adopted U.S. proposals to create a permanent business/private sector advisory body, to establish a private sector funded APEC Education Foundation, and to authorize a meeting of APEC transportation ministers to discuss the region's infrastructure.[9]

Following the ministerial meeting, APEC leaders held their second summit in Bogor and agreed to commit their nations to a specific timetable to implement free trade and investment. The Bogor Declaration stated:

> We further agree to announce our commitment to complete the achievement of our goal of free and open trade and investment in Asia Pacific no later than the year 2020. The pace of implementation will take into account the differing levels of economic development among APEC economies, with the industrialized economies achieving the goal of free and

open trade and investment no later than the year 2010 and developing economies no later than the year 2020.[10]

While in Indonesia, President Clinton and top administration officials further explained U.S. policies toward Asia.[11] Secretary of State Warren Christopher told APEC ministers that the president "understood that the security and prosperity of the United States in the coming century will be shaped in large measure by the stability and success of the Asia-Pacific region."   The United States thus viewed APEC from a long-term perspective, seeing the organization as having "a golden opportunity to help construct the architecture of a more prosperous, more integrated world."

President Clinton emphasized that "the United States will continue to exercise active leadership in the region" to help create "a post-Cold War world that is both safer and more prosperous" through activities such as APEC. "At the end of the Cold War," he said, "we are building a new framework for peace and prosperity that will take us into the future. It is imperative that the United States lead as we move toward this new century. That is our great opportunity, and that is the best way we can help all Americans toward a more prosperous future."

Clinton developed this theme in a speech to Asian-Pacific business leaders in Jakarta on November 16.[12] "Keeping America on the front lines of economic opportunity has been my first priority since I took office. We are pursuing a strategy to promote aggressive growth in the short run and in the long run."   This was being accomplished by "working hard to expand trade and investment" through "a vigorous export strategy" designed to tear down trade barriers and to actively promote the sale of American goods and services in other countries.[13]

Clinton said national security in the post-Cold War period must be defined not only in military but also in economic terms. In this regard, no region was more important to the United States than the Asian Pacific.

I have tried to make it clear to all the leaders of Asia that the United States will honor its commitments to Asian security. But it's also a fact, and a healthy one, that the balance of our relationship with Asia has tilted more and more toward trade. As a result of the efforts of the Asian people, the Asian economies are clearly the most dynamic and rapidly growing on Earth. Already they account for one-quarter of the world's output. Over the next five years the growth rate in Asia is projected to be over 50 percent higher than the growth rate in the mature economies of the G-7 countries.

This means expanding markets to those who have the most attractive products and services. Increasingly, we like to believe those products and services are American. One-third of our exports already go to Asia, supporting more than two million American jobs. Over the next decade, we estimate that if we are vigorous and effective, Asia could add more than 1.8 million jobs to the American economy, jobs that pay on average 13 percent above nonexport related jobs....These facts compel us to remain every more committed to deeper and deeper and deeper economic, political and security engagement in Asia.

"The importance of Asia to our future" the president said, "is what has animated the intense interest of the United States in the APEC meetings. APEC, for me and for our country, is a long-term commitment." Indirectly revealing his strategic goal toward Asia, Clinton said the United States hoped to use APEC "to give this incredibly diverse Asian Pacific region a common identity rooted in a common purpose, committed to free trade and investment."

Whether this long-term U.S. goal for the Asian-Pacific region will be realized remains uncertain. The forces opposing integration in Asia -- diverse cultures, different political and economic systems, historical animosities and suspicions, even competing regional organizations -- were substantial through 1995. (Clinton himself did not attend the November 1995 summit meeting in Osaka, Japan, because of domestic battles over the U.S. budget.) Nonetheless, the APEC process did highlight the "new web of human and commercial relationships" that were being formed and proved that "growing interdependence within the region is producing shared goals and aspirations and fostering a spirit of common purpose and of community among APEC members."[14]

Clinton's support for APEC demonstrated the linkage of economic, political, security, and ideological elements of U.S. policy toward Asia. Through a strategy of integration -- creating a community of shared values and objectives -- the administration sought to further all aspects of U.S. interests in the Asian Pacific.

North Korean Nuclear Threat

Unlike APEC, in which the administration could pursue a long-term vision of economic integration in the Pacific, President Clinton faced a serious immediate threat to U.S. security interests from North Korea, particularly its nuclear weapons program. The Clinton administration considered the North Korean nuclear bomb threat the most perilous legacy of the Cold War and the most serious threat to regional security in Asia.

In 1991 international pressure convinced Pyongyang to accept visits to its nuclear sites at Yongbyon by inspectors from the International Atomic Energy Agency (IAEA) as part of its obligations under the Nuclear Non-Proliferation Treaty (NPT). In late 1992, however, North Korea refused to allow IAEA inspectors to examine two facilities that were used to store nuclear waste. This refusal, coupled with discrepancies in DPRK data, resulted in IAEA demands that Pyongyang allow a "special inspection" of the Yongbyon sites, a request denied by North Korea. In March 1993 Pyongyang announced it was withdrawing from the NPT on June 12. The IAEA then informed the U.N. Security Council that North Korea "is in non-compliance" with the NPT and that "the Agency is not able to verify that there has been no diversion of nuclear material...to nuclear weapons or other explosive devices."[15] The Clinton administration began urgent talks with its allies, particularly Japan and South Korea, on how best to respond to the North Korean nuclear threat.

Coordinating moves with Tokyo and Seoul, Washington said it would take no further steps to improve ties with North Korea until the nuclear weapons issue was resolved. Japan halted its talks aimed at normalizing relations with Pyongyang, and South Korea refused to convene several South-North commissions established to discuss how to improve relations on the peninsula. China's help, considered vital because of close PRC-DPRK relations, was also enlisted. It was believed the PRC opposed North Korea's development of nuclear weapons and that Beijing had urged the DPRK to submit to IAEA inspections and not to withdraw from the NPT.[16] Beijing insisted, however, that the West continue its dialogue with Pyongyang and adamantly opposed U.N. sanctions against its North Korean ally.

The United States took the North Korean nuclear threat seriously in view of the credibility of the North's conventional threat. The DPRK had 1.1 million men under arms, and an additional 5 million with some reserve or militia training. About 65 percent of North Korean active duty forces were deployed near the DMZ in an offensive posture, spearheaded by some 3,000 main battle tanks. General Robert W. Riscassi, commander of U.S. forces in South Korea, told the Senate in 1993: "We are increasingly concerned that North Korea could slide into an attack as an uncontrolled consequence of total desperation or internal instability."

The 36,500 U.S. troops deployed in South Korea ensured that, if war did break out, the United States would immediately become involved.[17]

Because of the high risk and cost of a Korean conflict, the Clinton administration was willing to give some concessions to Pyongyang if it were willing to comply with IAEA standards. In early June 1993 Assistant Secretary of State Robert C. Gallucci met with North Korean First Vice Minister for Foreign Affairs Kang Sok Chu to discuss security matters. Such a high-level meeting with American officials had long been sought by North Korea.

Although the results of the first meeting were negligible, the North Korean delegation said the meetings "did not fail" and promised more talks before the June 12 deadline for the DPRK's withdrawal from the NPT.[18] In subsequent meetings North Korea signalled a willingness to implement an agreement with South Korea to bar the enrichment or reprocessing of fissile materials that could be used in nuclear weapons. In turn, the United States expressed willingness to halt its annual "Team Spirit" military exercises with the ROK, to pledge not to attack North Korea with nuclear weapons, and to promise international inspections of nuclear-related facilities in South Korea in exchange for such inspections in the North.[19]

At the last minute, North Korea agreed to suspend its withdrawal from the NPT, but it still refused to allow IAEA inspections of its facilities. The North Koreans said they wanted from the United States "assurances against the threat and use of force, including nuclear weapons," "mutual respect for each other's sovereignty," and "noninterference in each other's internal affairs." However, both the United States and the DPRK expressed support for a "nuclear-free Korean Peninsula," for a ROK-DPRK agreement to bar nuclear weapons work in both countries and to allow mutual inspections of each other's territory, and for the peaceful reunification of Korea. Pyongyang described the talks as a "turning point" in U.S.-North Korean relations.[20]

Negotiations between the United States and North Korea continued. On July 19 the two sides announced a limited agreement in Geneva. North Korea agreed to begin consultations with the IAEA over nuclear safeguards and to resume a dialogue with South Korea toward banning all nuclear weapons on the Korean peninsula. The United States said that, if these talks went well, it would help Pyongyang convert its graphite-core nuclear reactors to those cooled by light water, typical of most commercial nuclear power plants. Earlier, the United States had promised that productive DPRK talks with the IAEA would result in enhanced ties with the United States, including economic cooperation and substantial trade with Washington, Tokyo, and Seoul. The United States also agreed not to use force against North Korea, not to interfere in North Korean internal affairs, and to respect North Korea's sovereignty. If North Korea complied with all U.S. demands, Washington promised to end the "Team Spirit" military exercises.[21] At the end of July 1993, North Korea allowed IAEA inspectors to return to Yongbyon but not to inspect the two facilities suspected of containing evidence of diversion of plutonium for the DPRK's nuclear weapons program.

In addition to the nuclear issue, Washington used talks with North Korea to express opposition to Pyongyang's plans to export Scud-B, Scud-C, and Nodong-1 missiles to Iran, Libya, and Syria. Pyongyang was also believed to be transferring the technology and equipment necessary to enable these countries to build their own guided missiles. The range of the Nodong-1 would place all of Israel and even parts of Europe in danger from bases in Libya. All three missiles could carry nuclear warheads.[22]

The DPRK nuclear weapons program had important implications for the balance of power in Northeast Asia. If the North Korean nuclear threat could not be neutralized, it might cause South Korea and Japan to reconsider their no-nuclear policies. North Korea might also transfer nuclear weapons or technology to terrorist states such as Libya, Iran, Iraq, or Syria, further destabilizing the Middle East.

The critical importance of halting the North Korean nuclear program convinced the Clinton administration to continue its difficult negotiations with the DPRK, although many calls were heard for a preemptive military strike against Yongbyon. Former President Jimmy Carter played a useful role in averting a potential military crisis during his discussions with North Korean leaders in June 1994. Despite concern that U.S.-DPRK talks might be broken off after the sudden death of Kim Il Sung on July 8, the two sides resumed their dialogue after a period of North Korean mourning. In October 1994, after sixteen months of intensive negotiations, Washington and Pyongyang reached an important, if controversial, agreement on the Korean nuclear program.[23]

Under the agreement, North Korea halted the operation of its existing graphite reactor and stopped construction on two larger gas graphite reactors. In their place Pyongyang would receive from the United States and its South Korean and Japanese allies nuclear components for light water reactors whose plutonium would be less useful in fabricating nuclear weapons. To compensate North Korea for the loss of energy production in halting operation of its existing and projected nuclear reactors, the three allies would provide Pyongyang with 500,000 tons of heavy fuel oil annually.

The U.S.-DPRK "Agreed Framework" was said by Washington to "help achieve a long-standing and vital U.S. objective: an end to the threat of nuclear proliferation on the Korean Peninsula and provides the basis for more normal relations between North Korea and the rest of the world." If fully implemented, the agreement would bring the DPRK into compliance with the NPT and allow implementation of IAEA safeguards. From the U.S. perspective, the agreement was intended to terminate the North Korean nuclear program which, if fully operational, would produce sufficient plutonium for many nuclear weapons.[24]

The administration saw the Agreed Framework as a political as well as a nonproliferation agreement. Intended to "help integrate Pyongyang into the economic and political mainstream of East Asia," the agreement said the United States and the DPRK would establish diplomatic liaison offices in each other's capitals and move toward full diplomatic relations at an unspecified time in the future. The United States agreed to provide a "negative security assurance" pledging "not to use nuclear weapons against North Korea as long as it remains a member in good standing of the NPT regime." For its part, North Korea agreed to pursue its dialogue with South Korea and to implement the North-South Joint Declaration on the Denuclearization of the Korean Peninsula. The United States also agreed to reduce economic and financial restrictions on U.S. citizens wishing to deal with North Korea.

Whether the Agreed Framework would achieve its objectives remained unclear through the end of 1995. Its full implementation was in some doubt because North Korea refused to allow South Korea to participate in the construction of the replacement light-water reactors. The sourcing of the reactors and related technology had become mired in unpredictable North-South Korean political relations. In late 1995 the military situation along the DMZ also became tense, with DPRK military movements coinciding with a reported shortage of food for the North Korean people. Despite the U.S.-DPRK agreement on nuclear weapons, the peninsula remained the most serious security problem for President Clinton.

Clinton administration policies toward APEC and the DPRK demonstrated both the idealism and realism of U.S. strategy toward Asia. APEC represented the futurist vision of a community of market democracies led by the United States in the Asian-Pacific region. The community would share the benefits of free trade and pursue the common goals of security, stability, and economic development. In the case of the DPRK nuclear threat, the administration proved its pragmatic skills in defusing a potentially dangerous security issue. The long-term U.S. goal for North Korea, however, was similar to that held for APEC: integrating Pyongyang into the Asian-Pacific community as a way of more permanently resolving the DPRK threat to U.S. interests in Northeast Asia.

Pacific Command Posture Statement

One of the best summaries of U.S. security interests and theater military strategy in the Asian Pacific under the Clinton administration was the 1994 posture statement of Admiral Charles R. Larson, Commander in Chief, U.S. Pacific Forces (USCINCPAC).[25] Noting that U.S. economic, political, and security policies for the region enjoyed "excellent integration," Admiral Larson said:

> As the military component of that integrated approach, we have continued to refine the USPACOM [U.S. Pacific Command] strategy of Cooperative Engagement. Our strategy has evolved and matured to accommodate the reshaping of the strategic environment -- it's a cornerstone of the New Pacific Community. Our continued success in pursuing this strategy ensures the stability essential to a benign security environment, regional economic growth, and the enlargement of free markets and democracies -- all of which are clearly in the best interests of the United States.

The USCINCPAC posture statement affirmed that U.S. interests in the Asia-Pacific and the requirement for American leadership had not changed since the end of the Cold War. "Our interests have always included national survival, the peaceful resolution of regional conflicts, economic prosperity, cooperative relations with our friends and allies, and a stable and secure world order where free markets, human rights and democracies flourish." The major difference was that the United States no longer confronted "a single, irrefutable threat." Thus, U.S. "national survival, while always our first priority, is no longer `first among equals' as our nation's primary concern. We have expanded the scope of our national interests to include assistance and containment of failing states, the advancement of global economic cooperation, and the management of global challenges such as drugs, terrorism, refugees, overpopulation and environmental degradation." Consequently, "our strategic focus has shifted from a global threat to regional challenges and opportunities, from containment to a strategy of engagement."

The statement noted that since World War II American security policy had been "the linchpin" of Asian-Pacific stability. In the post-Cold War era, several emerging dangers in the region needed to be addressed by U.S. security policy. These included:

- *Regional dangers.* These stemmed from the region's tremendous diversity and "historic animosities, coupled with ethnic, ideological, territorial, and boundary disputes."
- *Proliferation dangers.* Eight nations in the region either had or were developing a ballistic missile capability, and twelve countries either had or were developing a biological or chemical weapons capability. Most major nations in Asia were modernizing their armed forces with sophisticated weapons.
- *Dangers to democracy.* Several newly democratic countries were "threatened by economic chaos or frustrated groups."
- *Economic dangers.* Protectionism and exclusion of the United States from the region were potential economic threats to U.S. interests.
- *Global challenges.* The Asia-Pacific region had many challenges such as population expansion, degradation of the environment, social displacement of large groups, AIDS, terrorism, narcotics trafficking, and refugee migration.

The posture statement noted that President Clinton had established a theater grand strategy in "a vision of a New Pacific Community built on shared strength, shared prosperity, and a shared commitment to democratic values and ideals." The security priorities for the New Pacific Community were also set by the president: continued forward-based American military presence; stronger efforts to combat proliferation of weapons of mass destruction and their advanced delivery systems; new regional security dialogues to complement U.S. bilateral security relationships; and support for democracy and more open societies.

Admiral Larson said: "As Commander in Chief, Pacific Command, I have a special role in the implementation of President Clinton's vision of a New Pacific Community. As the unified commander of our armed forces in the Pacific, I pursue a theater military strategy I call Cooperative Engagement." That strategy "aggressively employs the available means: forces, assets, funds, and programs; in three principal ways: forward presence, strong alliances, and crisis response; to achieve the desired ends of: engagement and participation in peace, deterrence and cooperation in crisis, and unilateral or multilateral victory in conflict." The admiral said, "If we must fight to protect our national interest, then we'll use the necessary force to achieve swift, decisive victory. But it's better to act with friends and allies as partners with a common stake in regional security; and it's best to prevent crises from arising by promoting cooperation and engagement."

The posture statement discussed U.S. bilateral security relations with key countries, notably Japan, South Korea, and China. In the case of Japan the U.S. bilateral security relationship "remains the cornerstone of U.S. security policy in the Asia-Pacific region. U.S. forces in Japan are a visible demonstration of our commitment to the peace and stability of the entire Asia-Pacific region and are available for short-notice deployment throughout the theater."

In regards to South Korea, the continued U.S. military presence in that country "is the single most visible indicator of U.S. commitment to the security of Korea and the long-term stability of Northeast Asia." The statement noted the United States remained "concerned over North Korea's nuclear weapons program and by its large conventional threat" and that the United States had "suspended EASI [East Asian Strategic Initiative] Phase II force reductions in Korea pending resolution of the nuclear issue."

The USCINCPAC's comments on China were drawn carefully. He said:

> China is at an historic crossroads. A stable, prosperous China which adheres to international standards of human rights and weapons proliferation is good for the region and for the world. We sincerely hope and expect that China will continue to make progress in that direction. At the same time, China faces potentially serious internal challenges, any of which could derail China's progress.
>
> We want a China that does not seek to impose hegemony or exclude the United States from the region. China and the United States have many areas of common interest upon which to build a much stronger relationship. The United States actively supports China's full integration into the international community. We want a China that freely accepts its full range of international responsibilities with respect to human rights, nuclear proliferation safeguards, and environment protection.
>
> China remains intransigent regarding regional issues it sees as bearing on sovereignty. China declares its claims in the South China Sea non-

negotiable while denying that others might have a legitimate basis for their claims. Beijing refuses to forswear the use of force regarding Taiwan's future. The United States does not take sides in the various territorial and historical disputes along China's borders. However, we do have significant interests involved. The use of force to resolve these disputes would be highly destabilizing to the region.

In the military arena, China continues to increase the pace and scope of its military modernization program. China's military is not a near-term threat to the United States. However, we do recognize the concerns of many regional nations about the power projection components of China's military modernization program. We seek sufficient transparency in China's strategic planning and procurement processes to reassure China's neighbors and ourselves that Beijing's military modernization program is limited to legitimate defensive needs and is peaceful in intent.

In the final analysis, I believe the best approach to dealing with China's continuing progress in the political, economic, and military arenas is to engage Beijing in a dialogue aimed at fostering cooperation and avoiding the development of a peer competitor in Asia.

Admiral Larson made a strong case for continued forward deployed U.S. forces in the Asia-Pacific as an unmistakable signal of American intentions to remain engaged in the region. "To build a New Pacific Community, the clearest imperative for the future is continued engagement in the region -- economic, diplomatic, and military. If we disengage others may attempt to fill the vacuum, inducing instability or a Pacific region inimical to our national interests." The admiral said, "The best way for us to deter regional aggression, perpetuate the region's robust economic growth, and promote our own economic and security interests is through forward presence and engagement....No diplomatic note, no political mission, no economic commission, conveys the same clear message of commitment as a visible U.S. military presence, active with our friends and vigilant for our interests."

In concluding his remarks, Admiral Larson emphasized the unique role played by the United States as the "honest broker" in the region.

We are the most trusted nation in the Asia-Pacific region, if not the world. Only the U.S. has both the capability and the credibility to play the "honest broker" between nervous neighbors and historic antagonists -- establishing a solid foundation for stability by making it clear that the most solid citizen in the neighborhood wants everybody to play by the rules. Only in this environment can we trade and prosper....Most importantly, forward presence demonstrates on a daily basis the continued U.S.

commitment to remain an Asia-Pacific power. Because of the tyranny of distance imposed by the Pacific and Indian Oceans, any claim we would have on being a legitimate Asia-Pacific power rings hollow in the absence of physical, tangible presence in the region.

Virtually every country in the Asia-Pacific region wants America to maintain its security presence in the region....I doubt that history has ever seen the situation enjoyed today by the United States in the Pacific. Throughout the region, there is a consistent appeal to the United States: "Don't leave us. You've been the stabilizing influence that offers the promise of a shared, bright future. Remain engaged."

Asia Policy in 1995

Assistant Secretary of State Winston Lord provided a valuable overview of U.S. policy toward the Asian Pacific in two presentations in January 1995.[26] These statements confirmed the continuity of administration policy with regional strategy defined during 1993 and 1994. The administration, he said, pursued three traditional American goals in Asia: security, prosperity, and freedom. During the Cold War, security was the top priority. In the post-Cold War period, however, the administration sought "to advance all our enduring interests at once, where possible, in turn, when necessary."

In pursuit of its goal of prosperity, the administration sought to open large markets, particularly in Japan and China, and to ensure America's economic place in the evolving Pacific community. Economics had become "a core element of our overall policy toward the Asia-Pacific." Lord said, "Active economic engagement helps to anchor America in the region not only in trade and investment but also in security and political terms."

This was done on several levels. Domestically, Clinton "made commercial diplomacy a top foreign policy priority," with U.S. government officials told to promote actively America's economic interests. Bilaterally, intensive negotiations were carried out with Japan, China, and other Asian countries to ensure fair trade and equal access for American goods and services. Regionally, progress was made through APEC to bring about an open and free trading system in the Asian Pacific. Globally, the administration used APEC, along with GATT, the new World Trade Organization, and free trade agreements in the Western Hemisphere, to promote global trade liberalization. APEC's Bogor

Declaration calling for free and open trade and investment by the year 2020 was acclaimed as a major administration success.

Security was a second goal in Asia. Lord stressed the important role of the United States in maintaining the region's balance of power. "Virtually every nation in the region wants us to remain engaged for strategic balance....It is in our interest to do so -- to maintain stability, to support our economic interests, and to bolster our diplomatic position." Key strategic bilateral relationships were maintained with Japan, China, Russia, and Vietnam.

"Our alliance with Japan remains crucial to our common defense and to our military balance in Asia." The administration had succeeded in insulating security ties from trade frictions, Lord said, but it did not feel "complacent about this critical partnership," calling it "the linchpin of our defense posture in Asia." U.S. efforts to enhance its global partnership with Japan were reflected in administration support for Japan's becoming a permanent member of the U.N. Security Council.

In regards to China, Lord said relations were crucial due to the PRC's size, nuclear power, and destiny "to become a global economic power."

> With the Chinese, we have followed a policy of comprehensive engagement, seeking progress on a broad agenda of issues through high level visits and working-level negotiations. Our strategic goal is to help integrate the Middle Kingdom into the international community, to encourage it to accept both the benefits and the obligations that come with interdependence and cooperation. Meanwhile, we have resumed a dialogue with China's military leaders to enhance regional confidence through greater transparency about China's intentions.

Although the United States had "modest success in securing China's cooperation on certain issues, including international peacekeeping, the North Korean nuclear issue, missile exports, narcotics, alien smuggling and regional security dialogues," there remained "differences over the sensitive issue of Taiwan, human rights and trade." Lord said the United States was "in a difficult phase" of the relationship, and he noted that one of the administration's major successes was strengthened ties with Taiwan.

With Russia, "our global approach of supporting reform and integration includes welcoming it into the Pacific Community." Lord said the United States had important regional security objectives with Vietnam which improved relations would promote. At the same time, "Vietnamese cooperation in accounting for missing servicemen remains the priority criterion for further progress in our bilateral relationship."

Although U.S. "alliance relationships and forward military presence form the foundations for our Asian security policy," Lord said the administration supported regional security discussions. "With relatively stable relations among the major nations in Asia, an unprecedented opportunity exists to build a more constructive pattern for the coming century. Thus, the Administration has explored new multilateral security dialogues in Asia. They will supplement, but not supplant, our alliances and forward military presence which we rigorously preserve."

The United States supported the establishment of the ASEAN Regional Forum (ARF), which had its first meeting in July 1994 with the United States, Canada, Japan, South Korea, Australia, New Zealand, China, Russia, Vietnam, Laos, the European Union, Papua New Guinea, and the six ASEAN states participating. The ARF was "the Pacific's first broadly based, consultative body concerned with security issues. In contrast to Cold War collective arrangements, the ARF is an inclusive group not directed against any country or bloc." Lord defined several ways in which ARF could further U.S. security interests: "We believe the ARF can play an important role in conveying governments' intentions, easing tensions, promoting transparency, developing confidence, constraining arms races, and cultivating habits of consultation and cooperation on security issues."

The United States also viewed Northeast Asia as a possible venue for multilateral security discussions. "Northeast Asia is both the area where great powers have clashed historically and the locus of the region's most urgent security challenges. Accordingly, there is a strong need for a sub-regional security dialogue." The Korean nuclear accord was pointed to as an example of a major administration success in Northeast Asia.

Freedom was the third traditional American goal in Asia supported by the Clinton administration. Lord acknowledged, "Promoting freedom while balancing other objectives is the most complex challenge -- conceptually and politically -- that we face." It was also "a quest in which we get the least international support." Lord defined the administration's modulated approach to human rights in Asia.

We are not on a crusade. We are not trying to impose our form of society or ideals. Each country must find its own way, consistent with history and culture. But international obligations to which countries have subscribed should be fulfilled. No government should violate the core value of human dignity, as articulated in the Universal Declaration of Human Rights. Each nation's citizens should have the chance to participate in the decisions that affect their lives, and the governments they elect should not be overturned by force....

Moreover, we appeal to countries's self-interest. Experience teaches that sustained economic development is more likely where government policies are transparent, where courts provide due process, where uncensored newspapers are free to expose corruption and to debate economic policy, and where business people can make independent decisions with free access to information....The foundation of open economies -- rights that protect contracts, property, and patents -- must be guaranteed by the rule of law.

Similarly, Lord said Americans should understand that "the defense of liberty is not merely an idealistic sojourn. Enlarging freedom serves our concrete national designs as well. The greatest threats to our security, and to Asia's, have long come from governments that flout the rule of law at home and reject the rule of international law abroad."

Looking to the future, Lord pointed to "the contours of commonality [that] are surfacing in the Pacific." Despite the region's diversity and its many challenges, the administration believed a sense of community was developing in the Pacific. This process of integration was being achieved through trade, telecommunications, transportation, and contact between regional business people, as well as the strengthening of regional governmental institutions such as APEC and ASEAN Regional Forum. The administration wanted to be part of and to help shape the emerging community of Asian-Pacific nations.

East Asia Strategic Initiative III

In February 1995 the Pentagon released a third major report in a series of East Asian strategic initiative documents explaining U.S. national security strategy toward the Asian Pacific through the year 2000.[27] In his statement introducing the EASI-III report, Secretary of Defense William J. Perry said the report highlighted the essential strategic themes of the Clinton administration:

- strengthening U.S. bilateral alliances while pursuing new opportunities presented by multilateral security dialogues
- maintaining forward deployment of U.S. forces and access and basing rights for U.S. and allied forces

- ensuring that security policies have the support of the American people and Congress
- promoting military-to-military contacts and security assistance
- halting the proliferation of weapons of mass destruction
- sharing responsibility for maintaining regional and global security.

EASI-III described the U.S. military presence in Asia as vital to the region's political stability and economic development: "Security is like oxygen: you do not tend to notice it until you begin to lose it. The American security presence has helped provide this `oxygen' for East Asian development....For the security and prosperity of today to be maintained for the next twenty years, the United States must remain engaged in Asia, committed to peace in the region, and dedicated to strengthening alliances and friendships." The report said U.S. interests in the region "are mutually-reinforcing: security is necessary for economic growth, security and growth make it more likely that human rights will be honored and democracy will emerge, and democratization makes international conflict less likely because democracies are unlikely to fight one another."

The U.S. national security strategy of engagement and enlargement had three central goals: "to enhance security by maintaining a strong defense capability and promoting cooperative security measures; to open foreign markets and spur global economic growth; and to promote democracy abroad." EASI-III said of East Asia: "nowhere are the strands of our three-part strategy more intertwined; nowhere is the need for continued engagement more evident."

Consistent with this national security strategy, the United States intended to pursue specific security objectives in the Asian Pacific, including:

- work with allies and friends to refocus U.S. security relations on new post-Cold War challenges
- strengthen the U.S. bilateral partnership with Japan which serves as the basic mechanism through which the two countries work together to promote regional and global security
- maintain the strong U.S. defense commitment to and ties with the Republic of Korea to deter aggression and preserve peace on the Korean peninsula
- work closely with Australia to pursue the numerous security objectives shared by the two allies
- engage China and support its constructive integration into the international community, including participation in global efforts to limit

proliferation of weapons of mass destruction and foster transparency in its defense policy and military activities

- fully implement the Agreed Framework on North Korea's nuclear program while standing ready to respond if North Korea does not meet its obligations or threatens U.S. allies
- work with Russia to develop mutually advantageous approaches that enhance regional stability
- contribute to maintaining peace in the Taiwan Strait
- work with ASEAN and others to explore new cooperative security approaches through the ASEAN Regional Forum
- encourage creation of a sub-regional security dialogue in Northeast Asia
- support efforts by countries in the region to strengthen democracy
- seek the fullest possible accounting of those missing in action from U.S. wars fought in Asia
- prevent the proliferation of weapons of mass destruction
- stem the flow of narcotics.

U.S. interests in Asia had remained "remarkably consistent over the past two centuries: peace and security; commercial access to the region; freedom of navigation; and the prevention of the rise of any hegemonic power or coalition." Likewise, U.S. military strategy since WWII had also been consistent: "to forward station forces to permanent bases, primarily in Japan, Korea and Southeast Asia." These forces were complemented "through the development of a range of bilateral security arrangements." EASI-III stated, "This approach continues to be appropriate because the leading states in the Asia-Pacific region have diverse threat perceptions and disparate cultures, histories, political systems, and levels of economic development."

Six core U.S. security commitments in the Asian Pacific would remain "inviolable" in the 1990s: the U.S.-Japan security treaty of September 8, 1951; U.S.-South Korean security treaty of October 1, 1953; U.S.-Australia security treaty of September 1, 1951; U.S.-Philippine security treaty of August 30, 1951; U.S.-Thailand security treaty of September 8, 1954; and Compact of Free Association with the Republic of the Marshall Islands, the Federated States of Micronesia, and the Republic of Palau of November 4, 1986.

The report noted that Asia's prosperity and stability were "vital to America's economic health and to the world's security." The U.S. military presence "guarantees the security of sea lanes vital to the flow of Middle East oil, serves to deter armed conflict in the region, and promotes regional cooperation." Most importantly, the U.S. military presence "denies political or economic control of the Asia-Pacific region by a rival, hostile power or coalition of powers, preventing any such group from having command over the vast resources, enormous wealth, and advanced technology of the Asia-Pacific region." The United States could ill afford a power vacuum in the Asian Pacific.

> If the United States does not provide the central, visible, stabilizing force in the Asia and Pacific region, it is quite possible that another nation might -- but not necessarily in a way that meets America's fundamental interests and those of our friends and allies....If the American presence in Asia were removed, the security of Asia would be imperiled, with consequences for Asia and America alike. Our ability to affect the course of events would be constrained, our markets and our interests would be jeopardized. To benefit from the growth and prosperity of the Asia-Pacific region, the United States must remain fully engaged economically, diplomatically, and militarily.

The report discussed several "key sub-regional challenges and opportunities" for U.S. security policy in Asia. These included (1) continued engagement with traditional friends and allies; (2) the exploration of multilateral security dialogue; (3) the enlargement of contact with countries not considered traditional U.S. friends; and (4) regional issues of concern to the United States.

In terms of engagement, by which was meant the modernizing and strengthening of existing U.S. alliances and friendships, the following relationships were especially noteworthy:

Japan. "There is no more important bilateral relationship than the one we have with Japan. It is fundamental to both our Pacific security policy and our global strategic objectives. Our security alliance with Japan is the linchpin of United States security policy in Asia." The U.S.-Japan relationship was seen throughout the region "as a major factor for securing stability in Asia." The relationship was "composed of three pillars -- our security alliance, political cooperation, and economics and trade." Economic tensions were the major challenge to the relationship. "We must not allow trade friction to undermine our security alliance, but if public support for the relationship is to be maintained over the long term, progress must continue to be made by both sides in addressing fundamental economic issues."

The Republic of Korea. "Our security relationship with the Republic of Korea continues to be central to the stability of the Korean Peninsula and Northeast Asia." Noting the long-term strategic importance of U.S. involvement in Northeast Asia, the report said, "Even after the North

Korean threat passes, the United States intends to maintain its strong defense alliance with the Republic of Korea, in the interest of regional security."

Australia. Australia was "an invaluable strategic partner [that] facilitates United States military activities and deployments in the region, through providing access to Australian ports, airfields and training facilities, through bilateral and multilateral exercises, and through vigorous programs for intelligence and scientific cooperation." Australia also "hosts and operates with the United States several joint facilities that make key contributions to United States, regional and global security."

ASEAN. "The United States shares an interest with these ASEAN countries in precluding Southeast Asia from becoming an area of strategic competition among regional powers." One U.S. goal was "to broaden our network of access and prepositioning arrangements throughout Southeast Asia to facilitate bilateral training, exercises, and interoperability" to enhance U.S. "ability to work with allies and friends in crises."

New Zealand. Although New Zealand became part of the ANZUS Treaty in 1951, it adopted policies in 1984 "which effectively prohibit ship visits under our policy of neither confirming nor denying the presence of nuclear weapons aboard specific ships or aircraft or by nuclear-propelled ships." Consequently, the United States suspended security cooperation with New Zealand in 1986. Since 1994, however, "we have upgraded our political and military contacts. It is our hope that in the future New Zealand will take the action necessary to restore its place in the ANZUS alliance."

Pacific Islands. "Many nations of the South Pacific Forum sit astride shipping lanes between the United States and our major trading partners in Southeast Asia, Australia and New Zealand." In addition to strong economic interests in the region, the United States had "specific legal responsibility for the defense of the strategically important United States territories of Guam and American Samoa, the Commonwealth of the Northern Marianas and, under the Compact of Free Association, for the Republic of the Marshall Islands, the Republic of Palau and the Federated States of Micronesia."

In terms of the exploration of new multilateral security opportunities, EASI-III said, "A significant new element of this Administration's Asian security policy has been constructive participation in and support for regional security dialogues." The study affirmed that U.S. participation in these dialogues was "an important element of our security engagement in the region." Since "relations among the major powers in Asia are more constructive than at any time in the past century," the post-Cold War period "provides an excellent and unique opportunity to shape a positive and cooperative security environment in the Asia-Pacific region."

Consequently, the United States supported ASEAN's 1993 proposal to create the ASEAN Regional Forum (ARF) "as Asia's first broadly based consultative body concerned with security issues. In contrast to Cold War collective defense against a common enemy, the ARF was conceived as an inclusive group not directed against any country." The report said:

> The United States believes the ARF can play a useful role in conveying governments' intentions, easing tensions, constraining arms races and cultivating habits of consultation and cooperation on security issues. We envision that the ARF will develop over time into an effective region-wide forum for enhancing preventive diplomacy and developing confidence-building measures. We believe that discussion of modest defense transparency measures would be a constructive area for future work. Discussions might include such measures as limited exchanges of defense data, the publication of defense white papers, and submission of information to the UN arms register. Efforts in areas such as disaster relief and peacekeeping could also help establish patterns of cooperation. Furthermore, the ARF presents an opportunity for a non-confrontational discussion of the relevance of democratization for regional security.

In addition to regional security discussions under ARF, the United States "believes that the unique long term security challenges in Northeast Asia argue strongly for the creation of a separate sub-regional security dialogue for Northeast Asia." The report noted that the United States had set the groundwork for such a forum by participating in a series of government/academic conferences with participants from Japan, South Korea, China, and Russia. North Korea had participated in the initial preparatory session.

In terms of the enlargement of contacts with countries that were not traditional friends of the United States, the EASI-III report specifically discussed China, Russia, and Vietnam. In the case of the PRC, "The rapid growth in China's material strength has raised the importance of China in the Asian security equation....It is thus essential for peace, stability, and economic growth in the Asia-Pacific region that China is stable and continues to develop friendly relations with its neighbors." Noting that China's real growth in defense expenditures over the past five years exceeded 40 percent and that the PLA was modernizing its forces across the spectrum of conventional and strategic programs, the report stated:

> China's military posture and development have a great impact on the expectations and behavior of other states in the region. Although China's leaders insist their military build-up is defensive and commensurate with China's overall economic growth, others in the region cannot be certain of China's intention, particularly in this period of leadership transition. China's military modernization effort is in an early stage, and its long-term goals are unclear. Moreover, it has territorial disputes with several neighboring states. Absent a better understanding of China's plans, capabilities and intentions, other Asian nations may feel a need to respond to China's growing military power. This will be particularly true as China modernizes its strategic forces, naval assets and other forces capable of power projection. The United States and China's neighbors would welcome greater transparency in China's defense programs, strategy and doctrine. [The United States] is enhancing its military dialogue with China in order to promote better mutual understanding, as well as greater transparency and trust.

The report said that "Russia is an Asia-Pacific regional power and an adverse shift in Moscow's policies would have an impact on Asia's security." In recent years, however, "Russia has contributed to international efforts toward peace, notably in connection with Cambodia and North Korea. Similarly, Russia has worked together with China to de-militarize their long contiguous border." If Moscow continues on this course, "Russia has a significant role to play in preventing the emergence of future security problems in Asia and the Pacific."

In the case of Vietnam, the report noted that the two nations established diplomatic liaison offices in January 1995 and that Americans can now can do business with Vietnam (as of February 1994). "Our major policy interest in Vietnam continues to be accounting for United States Service personnel missing in action from the war in Vietnam....At the same time, we remain interested in the protection of human rights in Vietnam [and] an interest in addressing narcotics issues." Predicting that Vietnam will play "an increasingly important role in the region," EASI-III said that Hanoi, along with Laos and Cambodia, probably will soon join ASEAN. (Vietnam did so in July 1995, the same month that Clinton established full diplomatic relations with Hanoi.)

The report identified several regional issues as security concerns to the United States. These included North Korea, Cambodia, territorial disputes, Taiwan, and proliferation.

North Korea. Although the October 1994 Agreed Framework offered hope in eventually ending the North Korean threat, "North Korea remains a source of unpredictability and potential danger for the region." The country's "excessive emphasis on military development at the expense of basic economic, political, and social development poses a threat to its neighbors." Moreover, "North Korea's history of aggression, threats to peace, and exports of missile technology have created a context in which its development of nuclear weapons would be an extremely dangerous threat to security on the Peninsula, in Asia and for global non-proliferation." At the same time, "North Korea's conventional military threat to the Republic of Korea has not abated, and requires continued vigilance and commitment of United States forces."

Cambodia. Cambodia "is emerging from two decades of war and chaos that followed the Khmer Rouge seizure of power in 1975." However, "since the formation of its new government [in 1993], Cambodia has made significant progress toward developing governing institutions, advancing respect for human rights, and establishing a market-oriented economy." Having participated in U.N. peacekeeping efforts in Cambodia since 1991, the United States would continue "to provide reconstruction and rehabilitation assistance, and non-lethal humanitarian assistance."

Territorial Disputes. Of the many territorial disputes in the Asian Pacific, the most serious involved the South China Sea, where the PRC, Taiwan, Vietnam, the Philippines, Malaysia, and Brunei claimed all or part of the islands and territorial waters, particularly around the Paracel Islands and the Spratly Islands. "The United States takes no position on the legal merits of the competing claims and is willing to assist in the peaceful resolution of the dispute." EASI-III warned, however, "the United States regards the high seas as an international commons. Our strategic interest in maintaining the lines of communication linking Southeast Asia, Northeast Asia and the Indian Ocean make it essential that we resist any maritime claims beyond those permitted by the Law of the Sea Convention."

Taiwan. The report said, "Peace in the Taiwan Strait has been the long-standing goal of our policy toward Taiwan. United States arms sales to Taiwan are designed to serve this end. We welcome the growing dialogue between Taipei and Beijing and applaud actions on both sides which increase the possibility of a peaceful resolution of the situation in the Taiwan Strait."

Proliferation Issues. "Weapons of mass destruction -- nuclear, biological, and chemical -- along with their delivery systems, pose a major threat to our security and that of our allies and other friendly nations. Our strategy seeks to stem the proliferation of such weapons and to develop an effective capability to deal with these threats." The report said the United States needed the Regional Theater Missile Defense System "to counter long range ballistic missile delivery systems in the inventory of many East Asian nations." Also, the United States needed "to maintain robust strategic nuclear forces while seeking to implement existing strategic arms agreements. Accordingly, the United States is reconfirming the nuclear umbrella it extends to our allies in the region, while pursuing bilateral and multilateral talks to cap, then reduce, weapons of mass destruction." According to the report, U.S. nonproliferation efforts in East Asia concentrated on North Korea and China.

EASI-III stressed the strategic importance of forward deployed U.S. forces in the Asian Pacific as "an essential element of regional security and America's global military posture." These forces ensured a rapid and flexible worldwide crisis response capability; discouraged the emergence of a regional hegemon; enhanced U.S. ability to influence a wide spectrum of important issues in the region; enabled significant economy of force by reducing the number of U.S. forces required to meet national security objectives; overcame the handicaps of time and distance presented by the vast Pacific Ocean; demonstrated to friends, allies, and potential enemies a tangible indication of the U.S. interest in the security of the entire region; conveyed a clear message of U.S. security commitments; contributed to trust in U.S. intentions to stand as guarantor of peace and security in Asia; enabled the United States to play the role of "honest broker" among Asian states distrustful of one another; enabled the United States to respond to regional crises and meet other military requirements; provided deterrence to regional threats while other U.S. forces responded to crises elsewhere; facilitated U.S. military response to crises in other parts of the world, particularly the Middle East; promoted democratic development in Asia by demonstrating the apolitical role played by the U.S. military; helped forge close ties with regional military leaders and to gain insight into their nations' military intentions; and maintained U.S. forces in a more cost effective way than if the same forces were stationed in the United States.

The report said: "To support our commitments in East Asia, we will maintain a force structure that requires approximately 100,000 personnel."

(This level was in place in 1994, a 25 percent reduction from the 135,000 U.S. personnel in Asia when the East Asian Strategic Initiative began in 1990.) Other than those afloat (approximately 26,000 personnel), most U.S. forward deployed forces were in Korea and Japan.

In large measure, the decision to maintain 100,000 personnel in Asia reflected U.S. determination not to withdraw additional forces from South Korea. "In light of the continuing conventional capability of North Korea, we have permanently halted a previously planned modest drawdown of our troops from South Korea." U.S. forces in Korea totalled about 37,000 and included an Army division and an Air Force combat wing. U.S. forces were in Korea not only to defeat a possible North Korean attack but, more importantly, to deter such an attack "by making it unmistakably clear that the United States would automatically and immediately be involved in any such conflict."

The majority of ground forces defending South Korea would be South Korean, not American. "This is in keeping with the United States' global strategy of contributing to regional security in ways that use our comparative advantages. In the case of defending the Republic of Korea, the United States has comparative advantages in naval and air forces and satellite and other intelligence. Thus, although United States ground forces will be needed for the foreseeable future to maintain the strongest possible deterrent, the United States will continue to shift gradually from a leading to a supporting role within the coalition." U.S. strategy envisioned a long-term forward presence on the Korean peninsula, regardless of the North Korean threat. "We envision a robust United States security relationship with the Republic of Korea to protect mutual security interests in the region, even if the threat from North Korea were to diminish."

The U.S. military presence in Japan served broad U.S. interests. "United States security policy in Asia and the Pacific relies on access to Japanese bases and Japanese support for United States operations. United States forces in Japan are committed to and prepared for not only the defense of Japan and other nearby United States interests, but to the preservation of peace and security in the entire Far East region. United States bases in Japan are well-located for rapid deployment to virtually any trouble spot in the region. Given the great distances associated with the Pacific theater, assured access to bases in Japan plays a critical role in our ability to deter and defeat aggression."

Because of the geostrategic importance of Japan, the United States deemed it essential to continue its military presence in that country. "In

Japan, we will continue to station a Marine Expeditionary Force on Okinawa, and will also continue to forward deploy an aircraft carrier battle group, and an amphibious ready group. We will also retain more than one wing of Air Force combat aircraft in Japan, and the Navy's Seventh Fleet will continue routine patrols of the Western Pacific." As Japan assumed a larger role in its own defense and that of surrounding waters, a division of roles and missions was possible. "Japan has concentrated on defense of the home islands and sea lane defense out to 1000 nautical miles while the United States has assumed responsibility for power projection and nuclear deterrence."

In contrast to forces based on Korean and Japanese territory, the U.S. military presence in Southeast Asia was much less visible. The presence was characterized by a wide range of military engagement and access arrangements, including maritime forces continuously afloat, rotational deployments, temporary deployments, formal and occasional access arrangements, informal agreements for aircraft transits and ship visits, commercial arrangements for ship and aircraft repair and maintenance, and various forms of defense cooperation ranging from intelligence sharing to personnel visits. Joint combined military exercises were also held frequently on both a large and small scale with the region's armed forces.

The high level of U.S. military activity in the Pacific was illustrated in the February 1995 USCINCPAC posture statement given to the Senate Armed Services Committee by Admiral Richard C. Macke. The admiral reported that, in implementing the Pacific Command's cooperative engagement strategy, the forces under USCINCPAC in 1994 participated in eighteen multilateral conferences with participants from thirty-six nations; held 416 staff talks in twenty-eight countries; held 192 joint/combined exercises in twenty countries; conducted seventy-seven humanitarian/civic action programs in twenty-three countries; and made 606 port visits in twenty-three countries.[28]

Conclusion

President Clinton's grand strategy toward the Asian Pacific was described in terms of building a new Pacific community, mostly comprised of market democracies but including nonmarket economies as well. This strategic goal was part of the administration's national strategy of engagement and enlargement. U.S. military forces in the Pacific pursued a strategy of cooperative engagement. U.S. regional strategy under Clinton encompassed a wide spectrum of security, diplomatic, economic, and ideological policies involving broad interaction with virtually all Asian nations. U.S. goals were quintessential American: security, free trade, and democracy. With minor exceptions, Clinton's comprehensive strategy was similar to that of George Bush, a reflection of continuity in U.S. interests in the Asia-Pacific.

The Bush-Clinton strategy of comprehensive engagement and enlargement in Asia included several interconnected components. Three of the components -- stability, deterrence, and balance of power -- were carried over from the Cold War and were designed to protect American national security interests in a traditional realpolitik fashion. The other three components of the strategy -- peaceful evolution, integration, and the expansion of market democracies -- reflected American idealism given renewed emphasis by victory in the Cold War. The rationale for these components can be summarized as follows:

Stability. The United States sought to preserve regional stability for several reasons. Stability in the Asian Pacific preserved a favorable international environment for the United States, enabling Washington to remain the preeminent power in the region and maximizing U.S. influence across the spectrum of American interests. Stability reduced opportunities for regional totalitarian governments to use force against their neighbors, thereby lowering the probability of the United States having to fight another major war in Asia.

Deterrence. The United States sought to deter aggression in the Asia-Pacific region from diverse sources, some identified (e.g., North Korea), some potential (e.g., China), and some unknown. Deterrence maintained by the United States contributed greatly to regional stability and allowed Asian countries to develop their economies and political institutions in a generally peaceful atmosphere. To achieve deterrence, the United States maintained a strong forward-based military presence in the Western Pacific, backed by overwhelming conventional and nuclear crisis response forces at home.

Balance of Power. The prevention of the rise of a regional hegemon continued to be in the vital interests of the United States. U.S. political, economic, and military policies were designed to maintain U.S. leadership in the region and to preclude the possibility of another power gaining control over Asian resources and directing them against the United States and its interests. The Bush and Clinton administrations retained the bilateral orientation of U.S. security strategy in Asia, but Clinton supplemented that bilateral approach with the exploration of new multilateral forums to discuss broad regional security issues. These forums were handicapped in that they rarely addressed a specific threat; however, multinational dialogue was a useful tool in encouraging integration and cooperation in the region. The forums also might have served as a political brake on the ambitions of regional powers such as China.

Peaceful Evolution. Although the United States enjoyed a favorable status quo in the Asia-Pacific, it recognized change was inevitable. U.S. strategy attempted to manage this change by creating an environment allowing for gradual, peaceful evolution in directions favorable to long-term U.S. interests: democracy, free markets, free trade, respect for human rights, and regional integration.

Integration. Mostly articulated in economic terms such as the APEC process, but with political, security, and ideological overtones, integration was a strategic initiative designed to draw the remaining socialist economies into regional trade and political institutions. This would help stabilize the international environment, expand trade opportunities, and further U.S. interests. A second, larger goal of integration was to build a sense of community in the Asian Pacific based on the principles of peace and stability, free trade, market economies, democracy, and respect for human dignity.

Expansion of Market Democracies. The Bush and Clinton administrations pursued the enlargement of the community of market democracies with great persistence in Asia. This was not only a moral mission for the United States, but also a strategic imperative based on certain assumptions: that western-style democratic systems were superior to other systems, that history was on the side of liberalism, and -- more pragmatically -- that democracies rarely became mortal enemies. Although this element of U.S. strategy was irritating at times to Asian countries taking pride in their own traditions, President Clinton in particular pursued this goal, in part because no single adversary threatened the survival of the United States in the post-Cold War period. Clinton also stressed the economic dimension of strategy far more than Bush, often giving commercial diplomacy top priority in bilateral relations. His policies emphasized the opening of large markets such as Japan and China and the continued leadership role of the United States in the evolving Asia-Pacific economic community.

Overall, Bush-Clinton strategies toward the Asian Pacific were well-conceived. Comprehensive, cooperative engagement was a robust strategy, with rational linkage between commitments and resources. Designed to preserve America's influence and strength well into the twenty-first century, the enlargement of the community of market democracies was an appropriate goal for the Asia-Pacific. Still, difficulties were encountered in establishing a proper balance between moral ends and practical means, and -- more importantly -- in justifying to Asian audiences America's leadership in this systemic transformation. President Bush had no difficulty in establishing U.S. leadership in Asia, but President Clinton's credibility in this regard was challenged throughout his administration.

Despite the strength of Bush-Clinton strategies toward Asia, several alternative strategic approaches exist which could be adopted by the United States either by choice or necessity. The next two chapters examine some of these strategic alternatives.

Notes

1. Winston Lord, "A New Pacific Community: Ten Goals for American Policy," opening statement at confirmation hearings for Assistant Secretary of State, Bureau of East Asian and Pacific Affairs, Senate Foreign Relations Committee, March 31, 1993, ms.

2. APEC was established by regional governments in 1989 for the purpose of promoting trade and investment in the Pacific Basin. In 1993 APEC had seventeen members: Australia, Brunei Darussalam, Canada, the People's Republic of China, Hong Kong, Indonesia, Japan, the Republic of Korea, Malaysia, Mexico, New Zealand, Papua New Guinea, the Republic of the Philippines, Singapore, Chinese Taipei (Taiwan, or the Republic of China), Thailand, and the United States of America.

3. "Remarks by the President to Students and Faculty of Waseda University" (Tokyo: The White House, Office of the Press Secretary, July 7, 1993).

4. "Remarks by the President in Address to the National Assembly of the Republic of Korea" (Seoul: The White House, Office of the Press Secretary, July 10, 1993).

5. "Statement of Secretary of State Warren Christopher at the ASEAN Post Ministerial Conference, Six-plus-Seven Open Session" (Singapore: U.S. Department of State, Office of the Spokesman, July 26, 1993).

6. Raphael Cung, "The United States and The Asia-Pacific Economic Cooperation Forum (APEC)," *Business America*, Vol. 114, No. 7 (April 5, 1993), pp. 2-4.

7. "Remarks by the President to Seattle APEC Host Committee" (Seattle: The White House, Office of the Press Secretary, November 19, 1993).

8. "Remarks by the President in Statement Regarding APEC Leader Meeting, Blake Island, Washington" (Seattle: The White House, Office of the Press Secretary, November 20, 1993).

9. See "Joint Statement of Asia-Pacific Economic Cooperation Ministerial Meeting," Jakarta, Indonesia, November 11-12, 1994. See also, Second Report of the Eminent Persons Group, *Achieving the APEC Vision: Free and Open Trade in the Asia Pacific* (Singapore: Asia-Pacific Economic Cooperation Secretariat, August 1994); and Pacific Business Forum, *A Business Blueprint for APEC: Strategies for Growth and Common Prosperity* (Singapore: Asia-Pacific Economic Cooperation Secretariat, October 1994).

10. See "APEC Economic Leaders' Declaration of Common Resolve," Bogor, Indonesia, November 15, 1994.

11. See "Press Conference by the President, Ambassador's Residence, Jakarta, Indonesia" (Jakarta: The White House, Office of the Press Secretary, November 14, 1994); and "Press Conference of the President, Jakarta Hilton, Jakarta, Indonesia" (Jakarta: The White House, Office of the Press Secretary, November 15, 1994). Administration policy also can be found in "Remarks by U.S. Secretary of State Warren Christopher at the APEC Ministerial, Jakarta Convention Center, Jakarta, Indonesia" (Jakarta: U.S. Department of State, Office of the Spokesman, November 11, 1994); "Press Conference with Secretary of State Warren Christopher, Secretary of Commerce Ron Brown, and Trade Representative Mickey Kantor at the Jakarta Convention Center, Jakarta, Indonesia" (Jakarta: U.S. Department of State, Office of the Spokesman, November 12, 1994); and "Remarks by U.S. Secretary of State Warren Christopher to the Jakarta American Chamber of Commerce" (Jakarta: U.S. Department of State, Office of the Spokesman, November 15, 1994).

12. "Remarks by the President to Members of U.S. Business Community and Pacific Business Leaders, Jakarta Convention Center, Jakarta, Indonesia" (Jakarta: The White House, Office of the Press Secretary, November 16, 1994).

13. A concurrent White House press release in Washington clearly drew the link between APEC and the administration's overall commercial strategy: "President Clinton arrived in office with a pledge to expand the economy and create American jobs. As part of the President's overall economic strategy, the Administration is aggressively pursuing an export strategy focused on opening markets to free and fair trade and helping American companies and American workers." The president's "infusion of energy and focus to the APEC" is one "of the building blocks to opening markets and creating a level playing field for American products." The White House pointed out that during President Clinton's and Commerce Secretary Ron Brown's trips to the Philippines, Malaysia, and Indonesia, nearly $41 billion in business deals had been negotiated, including fifteen agreements worth $40 billion in Indonesia. See "A Commercial Strategy for American Businesses and American Workers: The Clinton Administration and Asia" (Washington, D.C.: The White House, Office

of the Press Secretary, November 16, 1994.) In addition to the Indonesian contracts, five agreements worth $400 million were negotiated in the Philippines and two deals worth $250 million were struck in Malaysia.

14. See "Joint Statement of the Asia-Pacific Economic Cooperation Ministerial Meeting, November 17-19, 1993, Seattle, Washington."

15. *Washington Post*, April 2, 1993, p. A17.

16. *Washington Post*, March 24, 1993, p. A30; April 28, 1993, p. A13. Beijing's opposition to Pyongyang's nuclear program may have caused strains in PRC-DPRK relations. Several Chinese were reportedly shot by North Korean guards along the Yalu River border in the spring of 1993.

17. A Pentagon study completed during the last months of the Bush administration concluded that North Korea's conventional forces had become so strong that they could overwhelm South Korean defenses and take Seoul within two or three days. According to the study, U.S. forces involved in the initial defense effort would be overwhelmed. *Wall Street Journal*, May 24, 1993, p. A7.

18. *Washington Post*, June 5, 1993, p. A22.

19. *Washington Post*, June 11, 1993, p. A33.

20. "Joint Statement of the Democratic People's Republic of Korea and the United States of America (New York, June 11, 1993)," *Fact Sheet*, U.S. Arms Control and Disarmament Agency, Washington, D.C., June 22, 1993; see also *Washington Post*, June 12, 1993, p. A14.

21. *Washington Post*, July 17, 1993, p. A12; July 20, 1993, p. A14.

22. *Wall Street Journal*, July 19, 1993, p. A6.

23. See "U.S.-Democratic People's Republic of Korea Agreed Framework," *Fact Sheet*, U.S. Arms Control and Disarmament Agency, Geneva, Switzerland, October 21, 1994.

24. It takes between 2.2 and 17.6 pounds of plutonium to make a nuclear bomb, depending upon the design and concentration of the 239 isotope. *New York Times*, March 14, 1995, p. C1.

25. Admiral Charles R. Larson, "United States Pacific Command: Posture Statement, 1994" (Honolulu: United States Pacific Command, March 1994).

26. Winston Lord, "Building a Pacific Community: Statement before the Commonwealth Club, San Francisco, California, January 12, 1995" *U.S. Department of State Dispatch*, Vol. 6, No. 3 (January 16, 1995), pp. 34-40; Winston Lord, "U.S. Policy Toward East Asia and the Pacific," prepared statement given to the Asia and Pacific Affairs Subcommittee, House International Relations Committee, February 9, 1995, ms.

27. *United States Security Strategy for the East Asia-Pacific Region* (Washington, D.C.: Department of Defense, Office of International Security Affairs, February 1995).

28. "Statement of Admiral Richard C. Macke, U.S. Navy, Commander in Chief, United States Pacific Command," before the Senate Armed Services Committee, February 16, 1995, ms.

4

USCINCPAC Studies

This chapter reviews four studies done for the U.S. Commander-in-Chief of Pacific Forces (USCINCPAC), the senior military officer responsible for developing and implementing American security strategy toward the Asian-Pacific region.   Strategic studies sponsored by the USCINCPAC are usually well-developed with input from many sources, including government agencies and professional analysts.

To complement these officially sponsored studies, Chapter 5 will examine Asian-Pacific strategies suggested by independent scholars. These are often more imaginative than official studies, but sometimes lack depth of analysis and current data.   Taken together, however, the two sets of strategies provide a representative range of strategic options for the United States through the end of this century.   Both sets of strategies draw heavily from the 1989-1995 period, an unusually productive time for strategic thought due to the end of the Cold War and the need to find a strategy to replace containment.   Although many of the strategies reviewed in these two chapters focus on security, all are considered from the perspective of a regional strategy, incorporating not only military but also political, economic, and cultural dimensions.   A critique of the alternative approaches will occur in Chapter 6.

USPACOM Strategy for 2010

In October 1989 the U.S. Pacific Command (USPACOM) released a long-range study on U.S. strategy for the year 2010.[1]   Proving the inherent risks in such forecasts, the study contained many wrong assumptions, the most glaring of which was the continuation of the Soviet threat through 2010. Nonetheless, the report presented important arguments for an active U.S. strategy of deterrence and balance of power in the Pacific over the next twenty years.

Since the late nineteenth century, the study noted, "the U.S. grand strategy has been to prevent a single power, or coalition of powers, from dominating either Europe or Asia. It continues to be in the best interests of the U.S. to manage power relations in Asia so that no single power exercises hegemony." The United States was unique as the only Pacific power with political and security ties in Western Europe. Moreover, it interacted with more countries in Asia than any other nation. "This places the U.S. in a position of global leadership in the Asia-Pacific region."

The study predicted that in the near future Japan, China, and South Korea would be strong enough to counterbalance Russian expansionist ambitions in Asia. However, "the emergence of these newly powerful nations and the attendant balance of power shifts in Asia are changes to which U.S. strategy will have to be adapted." In addition, "recent and ongoing changes in [Russia], increasingly powerful Asian nations, and the spread of modern arms throughout the world will necessitate a transformation of U.S. security policy and strategy in the next two decades." The study recommended:

> As Asian nations become more powerful, the U.S. should exercise global leadership by pointing out that with increased power come increased regional security and burden sharing responsibilities. The U.S. can no longer afford to guarantee the security of the Asia-Pacific region unilaterally. Yet, the U.S. must lead the way toward a collective and cooperative security arrangement. The countries of the region must not find themselves having to accept the uncertainty and risks of a security environment in which no one has taken up the roles no longer being performed by the U.S.

According to the report, the pillars of U.S. strategy in the Asian Pacific were conventional and nuclear deterrence; forward defense and deployments; allied solidarity and burden sharing; worldwide linking of U.S. security interests; and favorable war termination. These strategic pillars were the means to achieve strategic objectives consistent with the principles contained in U.S. grand strategy. These strategic objectives were preventing single power or coalition dominance; preventing power instability; preserving U.S. economic security; preserving U.S. influence and access; and promoting extension of democracy.

Containment was no longer an adequate strategy in Asia, so the focus of U.S. strategy over the next decade had to be "deterrence and establishment of a balance of power among the new hierarchy of multiple powers. This means China and Japan must be prevented from becoming superpowers, the U.S. must achieve more favorable trade balances with the Asian market economies, and U.S. forces must maintain presence and access rights throughout as much of the Asia-Pacific region as possible."

The report said it was vital for the United States to maintain a worldwide presence, since this prevented regional hegemony and kept allies aligned with the United States. The forward based military presence in Asia assured China, Japan, and other countries that the United States was interested in regional defense. As Asia becomes more multipolar, "maintaining influence and access will become more difficult, yet not diminish in importance."

Ties with Japan would continue to be the most important economic, military, and strategic relationship the United States maintained in Asia. In regards to Japan's growing power, the report said,

> Japan will not become a superpower if it does not remilitarize and its forces remain insufficient for complete defense against another major power. The U.S. can abet that goal by tightening its strategic alliance with Japan, maintaining forward deployed forces and bases there, increasing the integration of the Japanese and U.S. military, [and] continuing to provide a nuclear umbrella. Japan should be encouraged to provide forces sufficient to protect its long sea lanes to Southwest Asia, yet it should be discouraged from developing a long range offensive strike capability.

The study pointed out that "continued U.S. provision of security for Japan tends to bound Japanese defense spending and ease Asian concerns about a remilitarized Japan."

In regards to China, the report recommended the United States "seek closer political, economic, and military ties in order to influence the direction of China's development away from military strength and toward economic prosperity."

The study predicted U.S. strategy in the Asia-Pacific region would continue to emphasize bilateral rather than multilateral relationships. However, the United States would need to continue its coalition strategy. The report said: "The U.S. cannot afford -- politically, economically, or militarily -- to play the role of policeman in Asia. Rather, it must rely on a coalition of democracies to preserve peace and economic prosperity." Because of its distance from Asia, the United States "must continue to deploy bases and forces within the regions of potential conflict." This means "the U.S. will continue to need forward deployed or rapidly deployable, strong, unified forces; robust alliances; and self-sufficient friends. If permanent overseas bases are no longer possible, then essential to U.S. strategy are extensive burden sharing and forces that are highly mobile, flexible, and ever-ready."

U.S. strategy required strong alliances. To this end, the study recommended the United States nurture a closer relationship with allies, especially Japan; increase burden sharing by allies; "proliferate the concepts and adoption of coalition warfare"; and explore all possibilities for alliances, such as seeing if India might be interested in closer ties with the United States to counter the rise of Islamic fundamentalism.

Historically, the study noted, "the U.S. has sought to maintain an Asian balance of power in which it is the predominant member with no other nation powerful enough to exercise regional hegemony. To maintain its position as the principal stabilizing power in Asia, the U.S. should strengthen its ties with China and ASEAN and discourage or impede" the following threats:

- a Sino-Russian bloc
- a threatening or dominant Japan
- emergence of other confounding powers
- revival of old rivalries
- strong military imbalances
- regional arms races.

The study recommended the U.S. military depart from its traditional roles and expand programs "to proliferate American political, ethical, and humanitarian values throughout the world."

Favoring a strong U.S. strategy of deterrence and balance of power through American-led coalitions, this study reflected the confidence felt by many Americans in the late 1980s that the United States would prevail in its global competition with the Soviet Union and that the Asian Pacific could be shaped in ways supportive of U.S. interests. The tone of the study was similar to that of a leaked 1992 Pentagon document outlining a $1.2 trillion strategy to prevent other nations from challenging U.S. primacy in the world. The document reportedly stated that the U.S. aim was "to discourage [other countries] from challenging our leadership or seeking to overturn the established political and economic order."[2] The

1989 USCINCPAC study applied a similar dominant leadership approach to U.S. strategy in Asia.

Cooperative Strategy and Comprehensive Security

Another USCINCPAC strategic study was made public in August 1991.[3] It proposed a "cooperative strategy in comprehensive security for the Asia-Pacific region" centered around U.S. relations with Japan. The study defined U.S. objectives in Asia as being to:

- maintain U.S. influence and access throughout the Asia-Pacific region
- provide reassurance of U.S. commitment to Asian nations
- deter acts of aggression
- maintain freedom of the seas
- prevent development of regional hegemonies
- thwart formation of regional economic blocs
- cooperate in efforts to solve regional problems such as poverty, environmental degradation, arms proliferation, terrorism, and drugs.

The study said U.S. Pacific Command (USPACOM) strategy could be summarized as "Being there -- and having lots of friends." Accordingly, the United States should do three things. First, "stay engaged in Asia, militarily, economically, and politically." Military engagement included "forward deployed forces, coalition warfare, combined exercises and training, security assistance, International Military Education and Training (IMET), and other similar programs." Economic engagement meant "taking part in programs such as APEC, ASEAN-U.S. Initiative, and other multilateral economic forums," as well as "aggressively pursuing economic opportunities throughout Asia." Political engagement meant "proliferating American political and humanitarian values throughout Asia." Second, as part of its strategy the United States should "keep Japan aligned with the U.S., [since] Japan is the predominant economic and technological power in Asia." And third, the United States should "serve as regional leader and honest broker," because the United States "is the only nation almost all Asian nations trust."

Focusing on U.S.-Japan relations, the study identified several constraints hampering the development of a positive relationship between the two nations. These included the "bashing" of both countries; the large U.S. budget and trade deficits; budgetary competition in the United

States between domestic needs and defense requirements; and an "emerging mood of new isolationism...gaining strength in some political corners of the U.S." The latter placed "a strong premium on the notion of `American first' in a narrow sense, and discounts the value of international engagement as fundamental to U.S. enlightened self-interest."

The study recommended the United States adopt a "cooperative strategy in comprehensive security for the Asia-Pacific region." The foundation of such a strategy would be the U.S.-Japan relationship. The strategy in turn would serve as "the fundamental rationale for the U.S.-Japan relationship in the post cold war era." The purpose of the strategy would be "to provide a secure, stable environment in the Asia-Pacific region that supports vigorous trade, business investment, economic cooperation, dynamic growth, and the development of democratic institutions."

The comprehensive nature of the strategy derived in part from Japan's own comprehensive strategy, developed by Tokyo in the early 1970s in response to the U.S. withdrawal from Vietnam and military reductions. In 1980 the Japanese government issued a "Report on Comprehensive National Security" stating that the adoption of the strategy had been necessary because of the decline in U.S. credibility in Asia. The Japanese report said: "In considering the question of Japan's security, the most fundamental change that took place in the 1970s is the termination of clear American supremacy in both military and economic spheres....As a result, U.S. military power is no longer able to provide its allies and friends with nearly full security."[4]

The Japanese concept of "comprehensive national security" was vague, but the term conveyed the notion that "national security encompasses a complex set of factors extending beyond military power to other dimensions: economic security, property, domestic tranquillity, and regional stability in East Asia. [In Japan] emphasis was placed on diplomacy and economic foreign policy; [however], the military dimension of security does remain a major component of the doctrine, and is still the foundation of the U.S.-Japan security relationship."

According to the report, the essence of a U.S. "cooperative strategy for comprehensive regional security" would be to work closely with Japan and other friendly Asian nations to serve mutual interests across a wide spectrum of national objectives. In terms of the United States and Japan, the strategy:

1. "provides U.S. access to geostrategically located bases in Asia to maintain forward U.S. presence, support U.S. military flexibility, and reassure Asian nations"
2. "gives Japan primary responsibility for conventional self defense to deter and resist unpredictable, contingency threats to the Japanese home islands and strategic accesses"
3. "continues U.S. responsibility for providing a nuclear umbrella and guaranteeing security of distant sea lanes." (The reported commented: "This adds little to U.S. defense costs in view of existing U.S. interests in Asia, and it eliminates the need for a large Japanese military buildup or out-of-area employment of combat forces -- neither of which is supported publicly in Japan or in Asia.")
4. "provides the opportunity for Japan to assume greater responsibility for non-military components of regional security, including financial aid and humanitarian programs that require the expenditure of Japanese sweat capital."

In order for the cooperative strategy for comprehensive regional security to work, the multidimensional aspects of U.S. relations with Japan and other Asian nations needed to be carefully coordinated in a national policy formulated in Washington. The key to the strategy, according to the report, was for U.S. policymakers to place multiple and often conflicting national policy objectives in Asia in a rational order of priority.

The 1991 USCINCPAC study emphasized coordinated use of political, economic, cultural, as well as military instruments to serve U.S. interests. The study concentrated on Japan as the key U.S. ally on which such a strategy should be built. In contrast to the 1989 USCINCPAC study, which stressed the role of the United States as the dominant military power in Asia, the 1991 study accentuated the importance of bilateral alliances and partnerships (especially with Japan) to achieve U.S. strategic objectives.

Credible Presence and Balance of Power

A third strategic approach was adopted by the Rand Corporation of Santa Monica, California, in a 1990 study undertaken on behalf of the USCINCPAC.[5] Rand emphasized the multifunctional role of American forward deployed forces and the detrimental impact a withdrawal of those forces would have on U.S. interests. Rand suggested that developing a regional grand strategy might not be appropriate for Asia given its diversity. Instead, the report sought to develop a rationale for maintaining a credible U.S. forward presence in the Western Pacific.

According to the study, enduring U.S. interests in the Asian Pacific were:

1. denying any single power or consortium of states domination within the region (including the prevention of further proliferation of nuclear weapons)
2. assuring unimpeded commercial and technical exchanges within the Pacific, with states not subject to coercion or threats of the use of force
3. encouragement of regimes committed to political openness and economic opportunity
4. seeking to maintain and enhance the incentives of regional states to collaborate with the United States in both politics and economics.

Rand observed that the need for the United States was "not necessarily for a new grand strategy design or for a comprehensive security structure (neither has existed in the Pacific in the past), but for crafting a security role appropriate to the regional conditions the United States seems likely to face, and to secure the interests that derive from those conditions." In defining the study's objectives, Rand said, "there is a need for an appropriate political concept to legitimate the U.S. military presence, both to help secure long-term American interests and to embed the American security role in a fully integrated regional policy. [As] the operative symbol of a continued American stake in the region...there is a need for an explicit argument about the purposes of [U.S.] military power."

Rand suggested the basic U.S. strategy should be "to maintain a presence that reassures allies, cautions potential adversaries, and avoids any implication of disengagement that might contribute to highly undesirable outcomes." Above all, there is need for credibility. The United States should

adapt future military deployments and security arrangements to a politically sustainable role for American forces in the Pacific. Thus, the United States must seek to define and maintain an appropriate level of engagement and military strength, even if this does not predict to a force posture of a specific size and configuration....By maintaining its forces at a credible level, the United States will convey to adversaries, allies, and nonaligned states its long-term stake in upholding stability and development in the Pacific.

The study said the uncertainties associated with the developing power equation in the Asian-Pacific region "underscore the critical role of American forces: the United States, and only the United States, can play a balancing role among the diverse power relationships that will emerge in the next quarter century. Even if this role is more political than operational, it cannot be performed in the absence of a credible level of U.S. military involvement."

According to Rand, the "central issue likely to transcend all others in Pacific basin security over the next quarter century [will be] the political-military role assumed by Japan." The United States should ensure that Japan does not again become a regional threat:

> The United States must seek to avoid Japanese recourse to an autonomous, offensive military capability. If Japan should arm in a manner that threatens the security of other regional states, other states will follow suit. Thus, the United States assumes a central role in determining future Japanese behavior, and hence regional responses to this behavior. The fact that the United States is now the region's preeminent military power decisively influences perceptions in the Pacific about Japanese power. Absent this U.S. role, Japan's economic and technological dominance would be far more threatening to the Pacific basin as a whole. This consideration makes it imperative that the United States maintain a closely integrated security relationship with Japan that does not invite Japan to move beyond its present responsibilities.

The study predicted that other challenges to regional stability might come from the enhancement of Chinese, Korean, Vietnamese, and Indian power. Smaller states do not want to be dominated by these major nations. Under these conditions, an "appropriate American security presence can help prevent a destabilizing military competition among fledgling major powers, as well as provide assurance against any state seeking to achieve predominant influence in the Pacific."

The study identified certain developments in the Asian Pacific that would be dangerous to U.S. interests. These included:

- a rupture in the current Japanese-American relationship
- an expansionist or increasingly hegemonic China that had enough nuclear capabilities to render extended deterrence by U.S. forces less credible
- a global or regional arms control environment that seriously limited U.S. freedom of action in protecting its security interests

- a militant, expansionist Indonesia that threatened to close lines of communication in its claimed territorial waters and air space
- a revolution in the Republic of Korea, with strong anti-U.S. overtones
- a nuclear-armed North Korea.

Given these considerations, Rand identified four broad strategic choices for the United States in the Pacific:

First, "augment U.S. forces in the region." The study concluded this strategic alternative was unlikely for budgetary reasons and unnecessary for security reasons. Therefore, it was rejected as a serious alternative.

Second, "continue the current strategic design" from a reduced posture. Under this approach, the only changes in U.S. forces would be in quantity but not in quality or in regional defense arrangements.

Third, "reduce the U.S. security role and presence and enter into arrangements that progressively shift the security burden to various regional states." Under this strategic option, the United States would play the role of "balancer and stabilizer," with a greatly reduced U.S. forward presence. To compensate, the United States might assist in the creation of regional or subregional defense collaboration arrangements.

Fourth, "a major retrenchment in the U.S. role in Pacific basin security." This strategic option would result in the United States maintaining a token presence in the region, with greater emphasis on nuclear deterrence and selected naval forces. There would be few forward deployed conventional forces. Asian nations would be responsible for their own security, except in instances where U.S. interests were directly attacked.

Rand did not make a recommendation among options 2, 3, or 4, leaving the decision to the USCINCPAC and civilian authorities. Significantly, the study dismissed the need for a grand strategy for Asia, instead emphasizing the practical importance of maintaining a credible U.S. military presence to ensure a favorable balance of power in the region. The key recommendations of the report were in essence arguments the USCINCPAC could use to justify the level of forces he deemed necessary to achieve his assigned responsibilities.

Regional Contingencies and Partnerships

A 1992 Rand study for the USCINCPAC defined more precisely a range of alternative peacetime and contingency operational strategies for the U.S. Pacific Command.[6] In this report Rand noted that U.S. forces in the Pacific, in addition to providing military security, helped "to underwrite the conditions necessary for national democratic political institutions to mature and for economic activity to prosper." The dilemma U.S. forces faced lay "in maintaining the necessary force capabilities in a time of shrinking defense budgets, possible base loss, and an erosion of economic competitiveness." In view of these constraints, "the U.S. must employ its limited resources wisely. If the U.S. cannot influence regional security with dominant, large forces, it must posture its smaller forces intelligently. One element of 'smart' posturing is ensuring that the U.S. provides those capabilities most necessary and suitable for a broad range of contingencies in an uncertain future."

The study contrasted the Cold War and post-Cold War security environments in the Asian-Pacific region: "In the past, it was possible to maintain a forward U.S. military presence in the Pacific to counter a real Soviet threat and thereby also have in place a military support structure that could provide immediate help to any security partners threatened by nonsuperpower neighbors." In the post-Cold War period, however, "a U.S. presence to support regional partners will have to be based more on the relevance of the U.S. force posture in preventing military conflict. U.S. security commitments can reduce incentives for expanded local military capabilities. However, the residual U.S. operations in the region must support the development of a combined capability in which the U.S. fights alongside regional security partners."

Absent the global Soviet threat, U.S. forces must be prepared to fight in a variety of potential conflicts, almost always in partnership with friends and allies. According to Rand, scenarios in which U.S. Pacific forces might be engaged include:

- Philippine Civil War
- Chinese Civil War
- Pan-Islamic Turmoil
- Spratly Islands War
- Indonesian Straits Denial
- Japanese Recovery of Northern Territories
- PRC Invasion of Southeast Asia
- India-Pakistan War
- PRC-Taiwan War
- Invasion of Saudi Oil Fields
- Renewal of Korean War
- Russia-U.S. War at Sea
- Japanese Pacific Empire.

The wide range of scenarios illustrated how the fundamental nature of U.S. security strategy had changed in the 1990s from focusing on a specific threat to being able to respond to a broader spectrum of conflicts in possibly unforeseen places and under unforeseen conditions.

Based on these scenarios, Rand developed five alternative postures for U.S. forces in the Pacific. Posture A was a continuation of the 1990 deployments of the Bush administration, with strong U.S. forces in South Korea, Japan, and in the continental United States (CONUS). In the next three postures, U.S. deployments were decreased by 15 percent to levels similar to the Clinton administration's defense program. Posture B maintained U.S. forces in their 1990 locations but at a 15 percent reduction in personnel. Posture C maintained the force level of Posture A but assumed almost all U.S. forces would be redeployed in a mid-Pacific strategy to U.S. sovereign or commonwealth territory such as Guam, Hawaii, and CONUS. Posture D was a swing posture, with the United States maintaining a permanent military presence in Southwest Asia drawn from USPACOM forces. Access to foreign bases in Asia would remain, but the level of the U.S. presence would be reduced significantly. Posture E assumed a major retrenchment from the region, with U.S. deployments reduced by 35 percent. Base access would remain the same, but the low-budget force would require significant changes both in U.S. security commitments and U.S. force levels in the Western Pacific and CONUS. In all cases, the study assumed the United States would continue its coalition strategy.

Regardless of the posture, Rand said, "The peacetime presence provided by U.S. forces in the Asian Pacific region is expensive, but we believe it contributes to peace and economic development in two ways: by providing visible evidence of U.S. interest and by maintaining properly trained forces, in adequate numbers, to back up explicit and implicit U.S. commitments to friends in the region." The presence of U.S. forces "may not have a significant direct effect on internal political actions, but the presence of capable U.S. forces in the region would certainly enter any aggressor state's calculations of risks and prospects for actions beyond its borders."

Rand evaluated each of the postures to determine its effectiveness in protecting U.S. security interests in the Asian Pacific. Posture A, while adequate to deal with most contingencies, was unlikely to be maintained because of budget considerations. It could not respond effectively to a surprise North Korean attack, to PRC ground forces attacking their land neighbors, or to a remilitarized Japan. (These weaknesses were true as well for the other postures.) The study emphasized: "A souring of the U.S.-Japan relationship would make the support of military operations in Northeast Asia much more difficult and would force a reevaluation of the U.S. ability to sustain full-time carrier presence in the Indian Ocean. Relations with the PRC, the former Soviet Union, and Vietnam are less important for this posture, since it includes an adequate military capability for responding to individual crises."

Posture B was suited for response to crises in Northeast Asia, but it reduced dramatically the U.S. presence in Southeast Asia and the Indian Ocean. It also made early warning of a conflict on the Korean peninsula essential. In general, however, "this posture provides adequate military capability for most scenarios and reduces some of the adverse impact of force reductions by maintaining a maximum forward presence."

Posture C reduced to a minimum the American forward presence by redeploying U.S. forces to the mid-Pacific. Rand considered the effectiveness of this posture "no better than marginal for all the scenarios considered." The primary damage would be to U.S. credibility and hence to deterrence. "It would be hard to argue that the U.S. has not fundamentally changed its role as an Asian Pacific power when force reductions are accompanied by withdrawal from forward bases. The result would almost certainly be a major realignment and rearrangement of regional security relationships." It would be difficult, according to the study, for any diplomatic, economic, or other U.S. policy to compensate for the deficiencies of this posture.

Posture D reduced U.S. forward presence in Northeast Asia and sent some of those forces to the Persian Gulf and Indian Ocean. Such redeployment of forces would signal a shift in U.S. priorities away from the Korean peninsula. Nonetheless, this posture could be sustained.

Posture E attempted to maintain a forward presence with dramatically fewer troops. Reductions in U.S. personnel were so severe that "the U.S. is likely to be perceived as maintaining only a facade of a posture." At the same time, however, "the war-fighting potential of Posture E is adequate for many of the scenarios," although "there is a point at which reductions in the overall U.S. force structure will significantly reduce U.S. war-fighting capabilities." Even with this posture, "the Pacific Rim scenarios we examined do not present threats that cannot be managed with the forces available, if adequate coalitions of regional partners can be developed and if sufficient time is available to deploy forces to forward areas."

The study pointed to several policy variables that would have an impact on U.S. strategy toward the Asian Pacific through the year 2000. These included budgetary pressures, the location of U.S. forces, perceptions of their effectiveness and responsiveness, the management of U.S. bilateral relationships, and how well the United States understood developments in the region.

One important factor was the development of a new U.S. grand strategy, which Rand referred to as "defense in combination with regional partners." The report stated, "Defining U.S. interests and a proportional engagement commensurate with the threat constitutes a *new* grand strategy, since it provides assurance that the U.S. commitment to regional security is as strong as ever." The report warned, however: "Even though a logical basis for this new strategy can be argued successfully, the U.S. must be aware that any such logic will be perceived by some as simply a rationalization for actions the U.S. is forced to take for reasons unrelated to national security."

Rand noted, "The emerging strategy -- defense in combination with regional partners -- will require a basing structure that allows the U.S. to routinely deploy forces and even preposition equipment and weapons outside U.S.-controlled facilities. The U.S. may be required to provide stronger assurances than in the past to gain the necessary access."

The report assumed reductions in U.S. forces in the Pacific. The adverse effects of those reductions might be minimized "by offsetting actions, such as a clearer definition of the threat, arms control to reduce the need for larger forces, and economic and political ties that reduce the likelihood that forces will be needed. The U.S. can also restructure the remaining forces to better support the rapid reintroduction of forces where it has chosen to draw down. Prepositioned materials and training with local forces are potentially high-payoff alternatives to the expense of maintaining a permanent physical presence."

The study reached several conclusions, including:

1. The size of the total U.S. active force structure is less important than maintaining a forward presence that is adequate for deterring potential opponents and for providing the stabilizing influence needed to reassure allies.
2. Planning for U.S. reinforcement needs to be oriented to Korea and the Persian Gulf.
3. Because the United States will have an insufficient number of carrier battle groups (CVBGs) to maintain historical levels of peacetime

presence, it must be innovative in considering substitute forces, including forces of other services, to provide a presence.

4. A major role of U.S. forces is to make regional arms races unnecessary.
5. Prepositioning and dual basing can pay big dividends both in presence and war-fighting effectiveness.

According to Rand, two fundamental pillars comprise the USPACOM operational strategy: (1) "maintain a *sufficient military presence* throughout the region to reduce the risk of war and to promote active U.S. participation in regional development"; and (2) provide forces configured to *complement coalition defense capabilities* in the event of regional conflict." While "some all-U.S. capability to respond must be retained," Rand said, "the focus for regional response planning should be combined operations with affected states." To implement this strategy, the United States should refine "the list of planning scenarios, the basis for judgments about the risk of war, and the ways in which U.S. involvement in regional military and economic planning contribute to risk reduction. It will also require further development of the concept of complementary coalition defense and will almost certainly mean less U.S. control because the U.S. will be contributing less. It also will require the U.S. to occasionally say, No, we do not see a need for U.S. involvement in that problem."

Based upon its analysis, Rand made several recommendations to the USCINCPAC:

1. Modify U.S. grand strategy. "The U.S. should modify its national security strategy to place greater emphasis on U.S. political and economic roles in regional security." The United States should no longer "go it alone" in the region, but rather change its strategy to reflect the fact that "threats exist, and they are numerous, but they are not as urgent as before, and the U.S. does not need to deal with them by itself."

2. Overhaul the CVBG deployment policy and patterns. The shrinking number of carrier battle groups means that, in the event of a crisis elsewhere, the United States might not have sufficient CVBGs to maintain its traditional presence in the Western Pacific.

3. Consider overseas home-porting of an additional CVBG. This would lower the ability of the Navy to surge in a crisis but would compensate for an otherwise reduced presence in the region.

4. Use more prepositioning. These facilities should be located in both Northeast Asia and Southeast Asia to enable airlifted troops to engage

rapidly. Such facilities might also compensate for the lowering of the numbers of ground forces in Northeast Asia.

5. Reexamine nuclear weapons policies. Other than noting "nuclear weapons proliferation will become an increasingly important issue," the Rand report did not elaborate on this topic.

6. Recognize that it is sometimes not of vital interest to the United States to become seriously engaged in a contingency that could prove to be major. The reduction in U.S. forces requires Washington to make distinctions between concerns and vital interests and that "other countries know it will not jump into every world problem."

7. Examine ready and rapidly deployable forces as a substitute for forward-deployed forces. Presence is vital to reduce the likelihood of conflict; however, budget constraints will limit the number of forces that can be forward deployed. Rapidly deployable forces from the continental United States may have to play a larger role in providing that presence.

In this study, Rand assumed that U.S. interests in Asia would remain the same, but that far fewer resources would be available to protect and serve those interests. At the same time, the nature of threats to U.S. interests had also undergone a profound change. These developments required a shift in U.S. strategy to one emphasizing partnership in the Pacific and a change in U.S. military posture to one providing credible presence but at a reduced level. Moreover, U.S. grand strategy should place greater emphasis on political and economic interaction with Asia to complement the U.S. military role in preserving regional security.

Conclusion

The USCINCPAC studies on strategic options for the United States in the Asian Pacific adopted four distinct approaches. The 1989 study proposed an assertive leadership role for the United States capitalizing on predominant U.S. power in the Pacific. The 1991 study proposed a more cooperative strategy focused on broad, comprehensive coordination with Japan and other U.S. allies. The 1990 Rand study did not recommend a specific strategy but argued that the many useful roles played by U.S. forces in the Pacific justified their continued forward deployment. The 1992 Rand study concentrated on various postures the USPACOM could adopt in the implementation of a strategy of "defense in combination with regional partners," essentially a strengthened coalition strategy focused on regional contingencies rather than a specific threat.

Many of the recommendations of these studies appeared in the East Asia strategic initiative (EASI) process, in which the Pentagon defined the essential role of the United States in Asia as "regional balancer, honest broker, and ultimate security guarantor,"[7] and in Clinton's strategy of engagement and enlargement to create a new Pacific community.

The next chapter examines strategic recommendations made by several independent analysts. Most of these are not as well developed as the USCINCPAC studies, but they are useful in expanding the conceptual framework of strategic options available to the United States in the Asian Pacific for the remainder of this century.

Notes

1. Karl Eulenstein, et al., *USPACOM Strategy for the Year 2010* (Camp H.M. Smith, Hawaii: USCINCPAC, Strategic Planning and Policy Directorate, October 11, 1989).

2. Quoted in James Chace, "The Pentagon's Superpower Fantasy," *New York Times*, March 16, 1992, p. A17.

3. Lee H. Endress, et al., *U.S.-Japan Security Relationship in the 1990s* (Camp H.M. Smith, Hawaii: USCINCPAC, Strategic Planning and Policy Directorate, Research and Analysis Division, August 1991).

4. Quoted in ibid., p. 26.

5. Jonathan D. Pollack and James A. Winnefeld, *U.S. Strategic Alternatives in a Changing Pacific* (Santa Monica: Rand Corporation, June 1990).

6. John Y. Schrader and James A. Winnefeld, *Understanding the Evolving U.S. Role in Pacific Rim Security: A Scenario-Based Analysis* (Santa Monica: Rand Corporation, 1992).

7. "Statement of Paul Wolfowitz, Under Secretary of Defense for Policy before the Senate Armed Services Committee," April 19, 1990, pp. 8-9, ms.

5

Alternative Strategies

This chapter provides an overview of strategic thought from nongovernment sources from 1991 through 1995. The survey is not intended to be exhaustive, but rather to highlight the diversity of opinion about future U.S. relations with the Asian Pacific. Emphasis is placed on the strategic approaches, not on their authors, although some scholars are mentioned by name as examples. For purposes of organization, the strategies are grouped under the categories of deterrence, balance of power, emerging threats, collective security and multilateralism, isolationism, and integration -- major themes that appear constantly in the literature.

Deterrence

One of the best arguments for a modified strategy of deterrence in East Asia was found in William Tow's study on extended deterrence in the Asian Pacific.[1] He noted several key differences between strategic perceptions in Washington and in most Asian capitals, especially during the Cold War.

A divergence has always existed between U.S. global deterrence strategy and those strategic objectives held to be most important by the United States' Asia-Pacific allies. Washington has been preoccupied with the nature and viability of the worldwide Soviet military threat and the challenge to the West. To most Asia-Pacific states, "security" is viewed as success in nation-building at home, the achievement of greater international influence, and the avoidance of involvement in regional or inter-regional conflict.

Tow argued that in the post-containment era the United States had to adjust its security strategy to accommodate the Asian perspective. In Asia there was a sense that security began at home. Markets and capital largely had replaced military instruments as the primary determinants of national power; economic forces rather than security considerations were the strategic factors given most attention. Asia was more concerned about resource competition than military competition.

Nonetheless, Tow said, many smaller Asian nations were worried about the United States reducing its military presence at the same time that China, Japan, India, and other major regional powers were building up their maritime power projection capabilities to secure needed resources. These developments, in turn, caused smaller nations to strengthen their military forces.

Tow believed one result of this process was an Asian perception of a decline in U.S. influence, credibility, and power. Most Asian countries did not want the United States to reduce its power and influence, but the decrease in U.S. military presence in the region after the Cold War forced Asian governments to adjust their strategies.

These negative perceptions could be reversed, according to Tow, because of the overall strength of the United States in Asia. "With its formidable maritime power and clear interests in retaining access to vitally important regional markets, the United States can and should contribute significantly to the preservation of Asia-Pacific stability and the implementation of confidence-building measures which could gradually supplant deterrence as the primary means of regional conflict avoidance."

To replace the Cold War strategy of extended deterrence, Tow proposed a strategy of "convergent deterrence" to give the United States a strong future role in Asia. Convergent deterrence blended strategic reassurance to Asian nations with some elements of extended deterrence. The U.S. goal was to become the *dominant* player in the region instead of the *predominant* player. This could be accomplished by integrating extended deterrence more effectively with regional priorities.

At the heart of convergent deterrence...is the requirement that Washington explore every opportunity to work with its Asia-Pacific allies in forging defense policies which meet both U.S. global and allied regional security objectives....It is critical that the United States be viewed as a continued force for positive and dynamic evolution in the world order and as a dependable agent for conflict resolution, helping to shape the Asia-Pacific's political and economic destiny.

Tow recommended the United States merge its global and regional strategies to ensure that both U.S. and Asian interests were served. His suggestions for a new U.S. strategy in the Pacific included:

1. The United States should define clearly under what circumstances and at what level it will use its nuclear, nonnuclear, or combination of these forces in regional conflicts to protect U.S. allies and American interests.
2. The Korean peninsula should continue to be viewed as a vital buffer to possible aggression against Japan from China, Russia, or North Korea.
3. The United States should consider missile defenses against China, Russia, and perhaps other powers in Northeast Asia.
4. Better communications and burden-sharing for sea lane control should be introduced in the Asian-Pacific region.
5. The United States should not only share defense burdens with its allies, but also share policy decisions in a move toward integrated joint strategic planning in the Pacific.
6. Areas of possible joint strategic planning could include U.S.-Japanese-South Korean cooperation on air interception missions, Malay-Singaporean-Indonesian military cooperation, coordination of intelligence sharing, and more joint military exercises.
7. More confidence-building measures should be adopted to replace deterrence as the principal means to maintain peace in the region.
8. The United States should have deployed, or deployable, forces in the Pacific to fulfill specific missions in order to rationalize the level of U.S. forces and lend credibility to U.S. commitments.
9. The United States should work to establish mutually acceptable norms for conflict resolution in the region as part of a strategy of "selective reassurance."

Tow's recommendations paralleled many of those found in the USCINCPAC studies. Both sets of proposals were transitional strategies designed to bridge the Cold War and the post-Cold War periods. Both emphasized the continued importance of deterrence. Both assumed U.S. strategy should utilize the existing military infrastructure in the Pacific, but it should refocus the U.S. alliance structure to serve regional as well as global security concerns. Both sets of strategies urged that greater attention be paid to the economic aspects of Asian security, and both justified continued U.S. forward deployments by emphasizing the multifaceted roles played by American military forces in Asia.

Balance of Power

Other strategic proposals emphasized a balance of power in Asia maintained through various geopolitical configurations. The post-Cold War suggestions of former President Richard Nixon, his national security advisor Henry Kissinger, and Richard Solomon, former assistant secretary of state for East Asian and Pacific affairs under President Bush, reflected this approach.

Richard Nixon believed U.S. relations with Asia, especially with Russia, China, and Japan, would determine the nature of the post-Cold War world.[2] Unfortunately, the United States "only pays attention to Asia in crisis." The key to Asian stability and prosperity was U.S. leadership, Nixon observed, especially the maintenance of a strong forward deployed U.S. military presence. "Without the U.S., Asia's future rests on a three-legged stool which is very unstable....Anyone who believes a China-Russia-Japan balance of power is stable is crazy." A strong U.S. military presence was necessary because all Asian nations, especially China, were increasing their military strength.

Nixon felt the American alliance with Japan was essential to a successful U.S. strategy in Asia. To let trade disputes interfere with geopolitical cooperation with Japan was "disastrous." At the same time, the United States had to retain its troops in Japan to prevent Tokyo from rearming to protect itself against Russia and China.

Nixon envisioned a classic balance of power strategy in which the United States, in alliance with Japan, would counterbalance the rising power of China and the remnants of Russian power in the Far East. Equally important, by retaining a military presence in Japan, the United States could deflect any move on the part of Tokyo to rearm and become a renewed threat to U.S. interests in Asia.

Henry Kissinger also recommended a balance of power strategy in Asia, one based on triangular U.S.-China-Japan relations.[3] He wrote: "Stability in East Asia demands a closer political relationship between Japan and the United States and that, in turn, requires a constructive Sino-American relationship. Without both of these elements, America's Asian policy will falter."

Because of strong Asian nationalism and the region's great diversity, an American presence in the Western Pacific was essential to avoid political chaos. "American disengagement, in whatever guise, would lead to disaster. The various Asian powers have such divergent purposes and traditions that America is needed to mitigate their competition and to develop cooperative purposes. Such an American role is desired by all of the Asian nations."

Due to the growing military strength of China and Korea and remaining Russian power in Asia, Kissinger said Japan no longer believed it could count on American protection in the post-Cold War period. This had led to increased Japanese military spending in an effort to become a more independent power, presenting a major challenge to U.S. strategy.

> The degree of Japanese autonomy and the kind of policy it supports depend crucially on the nature of Japanese-American relations. This imposes two requirements on the United States: to continue American engagement in Asia -- symbolized by an American military presence -- and to strengthen and redefine the Japanese-American alliance. When Japan and America formulate their policies in concert, Japan's incentive to build up its military power will be reduced, and its impact on the rest of Asia will be far less disturbing. Without an American presence, declarations of America's interest in Asia will not be believed, and Japan will be increasingly tempted into nationalist security and foreign policies.

Of equal importance for Asian stability was the U.S. relationship with China. "Above all," Kissinger noted, "the vitality of the Japanese alliance depends crucially on the nature of Sino-American relations....Good relations with China [are] absolutely essential to long-term good relations with Japan."

Nearly every country in Asia "looks to America to create a framework in which neither China nor Japan dominates." Kissinger observed, "China wants America to remain engaged in Asia for the same reason. It recognizes that America is needed to balance Japan and a possibly re-emerging Russia, and that America is in the best position to do so by maintaining close relations with each of these neighbors of China. But a policy of ties with countries simultaneously perceived as potential threats to Chinese security requires careful and regular synchronization of Sino-American relations."

Because of the strategic necessity of maintaining cooperative relations with Japan and China, Kissinger said the United States should not allow its concerns over Japan's trade surplus or human rights violations in

China to stand in the way of sound political and security policies toward these nations. As to the future, "Once America has redesigned its relations with China and Japan, it will be able to go beyond a set of bilateral relationships and enable the nations of Asia to communicate with each other in some larger framework. In the long run, an Asian Security Conference including Russia and the United States could be an important first step in that direction."

Elsewhere, Kissinger expressed alarm at deteriorating Sino-American relations under the Clinton administration. According to his analysis, the deterioration was based on Chinese fears that Clinton was pursuing a two-China strategy designed to contain China and American concerns that Beijing was deliberately challenging the United States on human rights and proliferation.[4]

Kissinger argued, "In the post-Cold War world, the United States remains in a powerful position to sustain Asian peace. Because the conflicts of the Asian nations with each other are more deep-seated than any disagreements they have with the United States, our bargaining position in a well-conceived policy is excellent -- an advantage reinforced by the fact that America provides the principal market for all Asian nations." Yet this advantage had been squandered by the Clinton administration because Washington had "become embroiled in conflicts with too many key Asian countries." The most serious of these disputes was with China.

> Stability in Asia is most likely if China and the United States cooperate. Conflict with China would encourage virulent nationalism all over the region. While an overbearing Chinese foreign policy could drive American foreign policy to such an expedient, nothing in the contemporary world calls for a policy of isolating China; the weight of our interests is in precisely the opposite direction.

> Both America and China have their own reasons for opposing the domination of Asia by a single hegemonic power. China wants the United States to help balance its relationships with powerful neighbors -- Japan, Russia and India -- at least until it is strong enough to do so on its own. America needs Chinese cooperation on these matters as well as on a peaceful evolution of the future of Taiwan and on the transfer of weapons technology. If these geopolitical issues move to the center of Sino-American relations, other issues such as human rights and nuclear proliferation will have a strategic context.

Kissinger urged Washington to be more sensitive to Chinese views on human rights and proliferation. "With a change of tone, I believe that progress on both proliferation and human rights -- especially the former -- is possible if the slide toward collision in the Taiwan Straits can be reversed." He warned that U.S. support for Taiwan, reflected in the granting of a visa to Taiwan President Lee Teng-hui to visit his alma mater at Cornell University in June 1995, was seen in Beijing as a two-China policy to divide and dominate China. "China would almost certainly prefer to resist a two-China policy by force than to be seen as acquiescing. And in such a conflict, America would be alone."

Kissinger believed U.S. strategy in Asia should be based on a well-conceived balance of power. This balance required cooperative U.S. relations with both China and Japan -- as well as with Russia -- to discourage hegemony, a dangerous arms race, and regional instability. As he told the *Far Eastern Economic Review* in November 1995:

> I think the drama of the next generation will be the attempt in Asia to develop [a balance of power system] because most of the major nations consider themselves competitors and not partners.
>
> In such a system, there are only two possible outcomes: hegemony or equilibrium. The European balance had to be achieved by relatively small countries in a relatively confined area. The Asian balance has to be carried out by continental countries in a vast area. That is the task of the next generation. And the task of the U.S. is to contribute to it and not to speak nonsense about a Pacific community that doesn't exist and that isn't going to come into being.[5]

A similar balance of power strategy was advocated by Richard Solomon, who believed "the future structure of East Asia -- to the extent that national governments will play a determining role -- is most likely to be shaped by the interaction of policies formulated in Washington and Beijing."[6]

Noting that the collapse of the Soviet Union and the breakdown in Sino-American relations after Tiananmen had "fundamentally altered the dynamic of international relations in Asia," Solomon was uncertain whether U.S.-PRC relations could be restored to normalcy. The Chinese were "highly ambivalent about the United States," holding the dual perception that China's economic development required close relations with America but that Washington was "the most likely power to stand in the way of China's claims to islands in the East China Sea and major portions of the South China Sea." Solomon observed:

> Virtually any leadership in Beijing will use the resources now being generated by the country's economic take-off to strengthen China's capabilities for regional -- and global -- leadership and for the pursuit of the country's national interests. The Chinese have always played for the long term; and unlike the Japanese, who have been content to pursue their interests in coalition with another major power (the United States), the Chinese are unlikely to be easy coalition partners of any other major power.

Solomon described Sino-American relations as fragile, since "Beijing will work methodically in the decades to come to regain China's position of international leadership that is assumed to be the country's inheritance and destiny" and since the United States will have lingering concerns over China's policies on Taiwan, market access, trade imbalances, nuclear and missile proliferation, human rights, and other issues. At best, the relationship was unpredictable and needed to be nurtured to avoid confrontation.

According to Solomon, "the most promising future one can anticipate for the coming period in East Asia is that of a loose balance of power among the states of the Strategic Quadrangle [China, Japan, Russia, and United States] embodying areas of political and economic cooperation -- with the U.S.-Japan alliance as the stabilizing core of the region." If this balance was to be achieved, the United States and China had to manage their relationship without conflict. "The United States can maximize its own interests," Solomon wrote, "if it is able to find common cause with all the major players of East Asia." On the other hand, if the United States misplayed its policies on issues such as human rights and trade, then Washington "could find itself the isolated party in the region."

The above balance of power strategies were based on cooperative U.S. relations with China and Japan. Other balance of power strategies, however, identify China and Japan as emerging threats to U.S. interests. Under these conditions, both Asian nations might be counterbalanced by closer U.S. ties with Moscow.

Michael Lind, for example, suggested an "Asia first" strategy that "would entail maintaining an economic and military balance between Japan and China, ending America's military agreement with Japan, increased cooperation with Russia on Asian affairs, forcing open Japan's and China's markets to U.S. goods, and dismantling NATO."[7]

Arguing that Japan and China would be the only global rivals to the United States in the next century, with China being the greatest military threat and Japan the greatest economic and technological threat, Lind said, "it is too early to tell whether Japan or China will be a greater challenge." However, the most prudent U.S. strategy would be "to keep its distance from both, weighing in on the side of the weaker whenever one grows overly strong."

Lind said the United States should withdraw most of its troops from Japan and replace the U.S.-Japan security treaty with agreements in which Japan would assume responsibility for its own defense. Regional defense would be shared between the United States and Japan on the basis of equal partners. At the same time, the United States should exert more economic pressure to open Japanese and Chinese markets to U.S. goods and services.

Since "it is in America's interest for there to be a moderately strong Russia to act as a military counterweight in Asia to Japan and China, we should continue to support Russia's territorial integrity and give it economic aid." However, the United States could not expect Russia's help in Asia if Washington antagonized Moscow in Europe. Hence, "we should replace NATO with a pan-European security organization that includes Russia and the U.S." Under Lind's strategy, Western Europeans would provide for Europe's defense, "permitting the U.S. to pull out most of its troops and end its implausible nuclear guarantee of Europe."

Thus, balance of power strategies can have quite different configurations in the Asian Pacific. Most of those reviewed here placed emphasis on the triangular U.S.-PRC-Japan relationship, but some were based on U.S. relations with Russia. Other balance of power configurations could place emphasis on U.S. relations with Vietnam, ASEAN, or India. The objective in each of the strategies is to align the United States with one or more major regional powers to prevent the rise of an Asian hegemon. Since only China, Japan, and Russia pose major potential threats to the United States in the post-Cold War period, it is widely believed the United States is well positioned to construct an effective balance of power regime in the Asia-Pacific.

China as a Threat

A number of strategies can be built on the assumption that China will become the principal security threat to the United States over the next several decades. Evidence supporting this assumption includes the rapid modernization of the PLA, possible hegemonic intentions, and a sharp rise in Chinese nationalism with anti-American overtones.

Militarily, China's conventional forces are considered threatening by most of its neighbors. New generations of warships are being built with improved blue water capabilities and advanced weapons systems, including *Luhu*-class destroyers and *Jiangwei*-class frigates. China has acquired Su-27 Flanker long-range multirole fighters, *Kilo*-class conventional submarines, T-72 main battle tanks, SA-10 surface-to-air missiles, and other advanced weapons and defense technology from Russia. China and Russia reportedly have held talks regarding the sale or joint production of MiG-29 Fulcrum and MiG-31 Foxhound fighters and Tu-22M Backfire bombers. Beijing may have obtained air-refuelling equipment and technology from either Iran or Israel and may be acquiring airborne early warning systems from either Russia or Israel. Other countries may be involved as well. There are persistent rumors of China's interest in acquiring an aircraft carrier.[8]

In terms of possible hegemony, Beijing has shown determination to back up some of its territorial claims by force, as seen recently in the Taiwan Strait and in the South China Sea. In February 1992 the PRC proclaimed a new law on its territorial waters that included the Spratly Islands in the South China Sea and the Senkaku Islands north of Taiwan. (China had earlier claimed the Paracel Islands north of the Spratlys as Chinese territory.) At the end of 1995 China had territorial disputes with Taiwan, Brunei, Malaysia, the Philippines, Vietnam, Russia, Japan, and India.

China's intention to use its new power projection capabilities to enforce territorial claims has convinced some analysts that China is entering a recurrent phase of historic hegemony. As B.A. Hamzah, assistant director-general of Malaysia's Institute of Strategic and International Studies, commented in 1992: "What we are now witnessing is a Pax Sinica in the making, in place of a reluctant Pax Americana and an impotent Russia."[9] A common viewpoint in Southeast Asia is that China has become the major focus of instability in the region.[10]

One explanation for the resurgence of China's ambitions is the rise of Chinese nationalism, which the ruling communist party (CCP) may be fanning to replace communism as the nation's ideological esprit de corps in the post-Deng Xiaoping transfer of political power.[11] The heightened sense of nationalism makes China very sensitive to real or imagined slights from other countries. The United States in particular has felt the ire of China, being accused repeatedly in 1995 of attempting to contain China to prevent it from becoming a major power. The CCP magazine *Outlook* in December 1995 said the United States was pursuing a "soft containment" strategy against China. According to the magazine, the Clinton strategy of "engagement" actually meant "infiltration" and efforts to force China to do things according to U.S. interests.[12] Hostile U.S. activities included:

- continued restriction of transfers of military and civilian technologies to China
- blocking China's entry into the World Trade Organization
- sale of offensive weapons to Taiwan and allowing Lee Teng-hui to visit the United States
- continued attacks on China's family planning policy
- spreading of the "China threat theory" to sow discord between China and its neighbors
- meeting with Tibet's exiled spiritual leader the Dali Lama.

Other examples of U.S. hostility pointed out by the Chinese include Washington's use of APEC to divide China from its neighbors and to justify the high level of U.S. military deployments in the Western Pacific, American opposition to China's hosting the 2000 Olympics, constant U.S. pressure on human rights and trade, American efforts to support political dissidents such as Wei Jingsheng, and the U.S. strategy of peaceful evolution designed to change China into a market democracy.

Since Tiananmen, an increasing number of Chinese officials see the United States as China's principal enemy. They think the United States wants to remain predominant in Asia and for this reason opposes China's emerging power. Some Chinese officials believe the United States has already begun a new Cold War with China as the target.[13]

Growing hostility toward the United States is accompanied by Chinese perceptions that Washington's influence and power are declining in the Asian-Pacific region. As one 1992 PRC report stated: "Although the end of the cold war has left the United States as the only superpower, its real power and position has very clearly been weakened." Reasons given for the U.S. decline included domestic social problems and a troubled economy, coupled with demands for a "change" in American politics from the general public.[14]

The rise of China's national power, signs of reemerging hegemony, and the growth of Chinese nationalism and anti-American sentiments are difficult forces for the United States to manage. Under a strategy of cooperative engagement, the Clinton administration repeatedly signalled its willingness to accommodate legitimate Chinese ambitions to be a great power. PRC aggressive activities in the South China Sea and Taiwan Straits were not referred to as "threats" but merely cause for "concern."[15]

But cooperative engagement could not obscure the many problems the United States had with China. In addition to the PLA's modernization of power projection forces and menacing military activities near Taiwan and in the South China Sea, these problems included Beijing's human rights violations, continued nuclear testing, the sale of missiles and nuclear technology to Pakistan and Middle Eastern countries, and a swelling trade surplus with the United States. The surplus approached $35 billion in 1995 and was projected to be greater than Japan's trade surplus around the turn of the century.[16]

These security, political, human rights, and economic issues were accompanied by a fundamental ideological schism between the United States and China. The United States wanted to create a new world order characterized by free markets, open trade, democracy, and respect for human rights. The Chinese sought a new international order in which each country pursued its own political, economic, and cultural development. U.S. efforts to mold the international system according to its values were seen by Beijing as interference in the internal affairs of sovereign states.

Clearly, the PRC is not interested in preserving the status quo in Asia. With the end of the Cold War and the withdrawal of most Soviet and some American forces from Asia, Beijing has an opportunity to expand its influence in a region historically part of China's sphere of influence. According to Samuel Huntington, if China continues its spectacular growth over the next decade, it will constitute the "single most destabilizing event of the post-Cold War era." And in the next century, he warns, China is the nation "most likely to challenge the West for global influence."[17]

At what point do Chinese ambitions cease to be "concerns" and become "threats" to regional peace and stability? Historically, a fundamental U.S. strategic objective in Asia has been to preserve a favorable balance of power in which no other nation dominated the region. Given China's growth in national power over the past decade, an increasing number of American strategists believe the United States must be wary of Chinese ambitions. Jonathan Pollack, for example, has suggested Washington follow a "hedge strategy" in which the United States continues to engage China but keeps its guard up in case the PRC becomes too aggressive.[18]

Fearing a Sino-American confrontation as the two powers maneuver to find a new strategic balance in Asia, some strategists think the United States should take more active steps to ensure that China does not become too strong. One way might be to increase U.S. arms sales to Taiwan. In 1992, for example, the Bush administration sold Taiwan 150 F-16A/B fighters partly on the grounds that Beijing's purchase of Soviet Su-27s had upset the balance of power in the Taiwan Strait.[19] Subsequently, both the Bush and Clinton administrations approved substantive defense sales to Taiwan, including advanced antisubmarine helicopters, antisubmarine frigates, Harpoon antiship missiles, Patriot missiles, heavy tanks, early warning aircraft, modern ground radar systems, and other weapons and defense technology. China's increased military pressure on Taiwan following President Lee Teng-hui's visit to the United States in 1995 may result in still higher levels of arms sales to Taiwan.[20]

Another way to counterbalance PRC power might be closer U.S. ties with Vietnam, China's neighboring rival in Southeast Asia. President Clinton extended full diplomatic relations to Vietnam in June 1995. In recommending this step, Senator John McCain said:

> If decentralization and other political dynamics within China today do not lead to the systemic reform of the regime and the restraint of Chinese imperialism, the United States will likely confront China as our number one security problem.
>
> It is, therefore, absolutely in our national security interests to have an economically viable Vietnam strong enough to resist, in concert with its neighbors, the heavy-handed tactics of its great power neighbor. That reason, more than any other, urges the normalization of our relations and makes Vietnam's membership in the Association of Southeast Asian Nations, and the increasingly responsible role Hanoi is playing in regional affairs, a very welcome development.[21]

Five factors are critical in assessing a possible PRC threat to the United States: Beijing's intentions, PLA capabilities, America's definition of its interests in Asia, U.S. intentions to defend those interests, and U.S. military capabilities in the Pacific. A number of scenarios can be constructed based on these variables, but broad parameters are fairly easy to establish.

A worst case scenario for the year 2000 might be as follows: China's intentions were hostile to U.S. interests; the PLA possessed strong power projection capabilities; Washington's willingness to protect its interests was weak; American forces in Asia were minimal. A best case scenario might be: China's intentions were friendly to the United States; the PLA was moderately strong but postured for defensive purposes; Washington was determined to defend its interests in Asia; the U.S. military presence in the Western Pacific was overwhelming. A more likely scenario would fall somewhere in between: China continued to expand its influence in regional and global affairs; Beijing was willing to use force, if necessary, to protect Chinese sovereignty and territory; the PRC possessed one of the most powerful armed forces in Asia, but it was weak in key areas of modernization; the United States continued to define its interests broadly in Asia, and Washington was willing to use its national power to advance those interests; U.S. military capabilities were overwhelming at sea and in the air, but they were not designed for a conventional land war on the Asian continent.

Under these basic scenarios, the United States could pursue a number of alternative strategies. For example:

- The United States could adopt a strategy of retreat from Asia. American strength might not be sufficient to oppose the PRC and U.S. credibility might be too low for Asian nations to risk opposing Beijing. The United States would be forced to accept a major realignment of the balance of power in Asia. China would be the acknowledged dominant power in the region, U.S. influence would decline precipitously, and the traditional U.S. policy of ensuring that no Asian nation exercised hegemony would be abandoned.

- The United States could pursue a strategy to topple the CCP regime. With superior power and political influence, the United States could attempt to replace the Chinese communist government with a pro-Western, democratic government. This strategy would probably include substantial support to Taiwan and to anti-government movements in China, Tibet, and Xinjiang.

- The United States could pursue a strategy of containment of China, imposed unilaterally or in cooperation with Asian and European allies.

- The United States could continue its strategy of peaceful evolution, seeking through expanded contact with the West a gradual change of China's political and economic systems into a market democracy.

- The United States could adopt a strategy of accommodation, not interfering with China as it became a major power in Asia and making the necessary adjustments in U.S. interests and policies to avoid a direct conflict with Beijing.

- The United States could pursue a strategy of confrontation, determining China to be an enemy and preparing for military conflict in which

American forces would defeat the PLA and impose by force a limitation on Beijing's great power ambitions.
- The United States could pursue a strategy of manipulation, using ad hoc rewards and punishments in an attempt to channel PRC policies in directions favoring U.S. interests in Asia.

In theory, U.S. alternative strategies toward China are many, but in reality U.S. strategic options may be limited. Ultimately, a highly critical factor may be China's nuclear weapons and ballistic missiles. While not yet a superpower, China may become so within two decades. At that time, targets within the continental United States may be vulnerable to PRC strategic weapons. When China possesses these capabilities, many of the same considerations that governed U.S. relations with the former Soviet Union may govern U.S. relations with Beijing. These considerations might include the following around the year 2005:

- China would pose a strategic and conventional threat to the vital security interests of the United States.
- The Chinese threat should be countered, contained, and defeated if necessary.
- It would not be in the U.S. interest to go to war with China, especially under conditions in which nuclear weapons might be used.
- U.S. strategy should deter China, but it should not precipitate a direct Sino-American conflict.
- High-level U.S. interaction with Beijing would be necessary to ensure mutual understanding and, hopefully, to lower PRC incentives to confront Washington militarily.

In the final analysis, the nature of the Chinese government and its policies toward the United States probably will be the most important determinants of whether China is considered an enemy, friend, or rival power in the next century. U.S. strategy and policy toward Beijing will closely reflect that determination.

In sum, at the present time the PRC is becoming a stronger country and Chinese nationalism is on the rise. Increasingly, Beijing believes U.S. forces are in the Pacific to contain China, not protect it from Russia or Japan. PRC leaders feel they must recover Chinese territories lost during a century of humiliation by Western, Russian, and Japanese imperialism. A more assertive Chinese foreign policy is justified from the point of view of many Chinese (and understandable to Westerners in the context of leadership transition in the CCP), but PRC policies increasingly threaten U.S. interests in preserving a balance of power in

Asia and in ensuring that no other power dominates the region. The United States and China are two major powers with spheres of influence that increasingly overlap. Redefining a stable border between these spheres will be difficult and the subject of much strategic debate in years to come.

Future Role of Japan

Almost all U.S. strategic options for Asia place great emphasis on the role of Japan. Under Presidents Reagan, Bush, and Clinton, the United States made concerted efforts to encourage Japan to play a larger role in regional and global affairs, one more commensurate with its economic stature. Secretary of State James Baker, for example, said in November 1991 that the United States wanted Japan to play a larger leadership role not just in economic affairs but also in building democracy, promoting respect for human rights, stopping the proliferation of weapons of mass destruction, and meeting the challenges of the environment, narcotics, and refugees. Baker said, "Japan should step forward as a leader in confronting global issues rather then relying on *gaiatsu* -- foreign pressure -- to justify decisions on economics or security affairs that are in its own interests."[22] One of the foreign policy objectives of the Clinton administration was Japan's permanent membership in the U.N. Security Council.[23]

U.S. plans for global partnership with Japan were part of a larger strategic vision of broader cooperation with U.S. friends and allies in the aftermath of the Cold War. The Bush administration adopted the principle that there should be a clearer division of labor between the United States and its close friends in Asia in order to promote mutual interests and common values. Japan was the centerpiece of this vision.

Clinton's call for the building of a "new Pacific community" continued the Bush plan to build a new partnership in Asia centered around global cooperation between Washington and Tokyo. It was believed that Japan must play a central role in a strategy of Asian-Pacific integration because of Tokyo's vast economic presence in Asia and its vital position as a base for forward U.S. military deployments serving the entire region.

It is an article of faith among most analysts that Japan must remain a U.S. ally. In the post-Cold War period, however, the U.S.-Japan security relationship has come under intense pressure. During its first two years in office, Clinton administration policy toward Japan was characterized by unrelenting demands that Tokyo open its markets to U.S. goods and services, an approach that resulted both in concessions and resentment. Partly in reaction to the strain in U.S.-Japan relations, in 1994 there were increased calls in Japan for a more autonomous Japanese military as a hedge against possible future reduction of U.S. interests in Japan. These calls raised concern in Washington that the security alliance might be unravelling, a concern greatly heightened by the huge protests against the U.S. military presence in Japan and Okinawa precipitated by the rape of an Okinawan girl by American Marines in the fall of 1995. This public outcry drove home the fragility of U.S.-Japan security ties in the absence of a compelling mutual threat such as the former Soviet Union.

Thus, while most U.S. strategies assume the continuation of Japan's role as the pivotal American ally in the Asian Pacific, other strategic options are being considered. A number of American analysts feel the U.S.-Japan alliance has outlived its usefulness and should be changed or discarded. Others view Japan -- not China -- as the most dangerous potential threat to long-term U.S. interests in Asia.

Those who see Japan as an emerging threat can point to several factors. First, for much of the past century Japan has been the major threat to U.S. interests in Asia and the Pacific. Demonstrating imperialist tendencies in the past, Japan remains dependent on overseas markets for vital resources and trade. China and Russia, the two other major potential threats to U.S. interests in East Asia, are large continental powers more self-reliant economically than either Japan or the United States. Since these geopolitical circumstances will not change, the same pattern of intense U.S.-Japanese competition over Asian markets and raw materials that characterized prewar relations may distinguish future relations between the two countries.

Second, Japan's industrial and technological capabilities are sufficiently robust to challenge the United States militarily. Japan has the world's second largest economy, and while its defense expenditures hover around 1 percent of GNP, its defense budget of about $42 billion in 1994 was the second largest after the United States and nearly 60 percent greater than the estimated $27 billion defense expenditures of China.[24]

Third, the United States and Japan have a long history of misunderstanding, an important contributing factor to the outbreak of World War II in the Pacific. Despite the fact that both sides usually seek accommodation, misunderstanding of motives and intentions between Americans and Japanese is still common today.

Fourth, geography places Japan and the United States in unavoidable competition in the Western Pacific. The two countries are major powers with overlapping spheres of influence and competing national interests. The United States and Great Britain eventually became steadfast allies across the Atlantic, but in the eighteenth and nineteenth centuries the two sides fought two wars and had innumerable armed confrontations. The U.S.-U.K. partnership eventually prospered, in large part because of cultural affinity. Japan is central to U.S. security, political, and economic interests in Asia; and Tokyo finds its security, political, and economic interests served by alliance with the United States. However, cultural affinity between the two nations is minimal, making a true partnership across the Pacific much more problematical.

Therefore, there is a possibility (deemed remote by most observers but likely by some) of the United States and Japan once again becoming enemies, despite their mutual interest in maintaining an alliance. Strategies which assume future U.S.-Japanese enmity include the following general approaches:

- The United States could align with China or Russia to counterbalance Japan and contain its expansion.
- The United States could retreat from the Western Pacific, allowing Japan to build the region's most powerful navy and to assume the role of protector of the sea lanes.
- The United States could prepare for another war with Japan, expecting once again to defeat Tokyo and thereby regain American predominance in the region.

The implications of hostile U.S. relations with Japan are enormous: American bases in Japan would not be available; more U.S. aircraft carrier battle groups would have to be built to project the same amount of U.S. power into the Western Pacific; Washington would have to work hard to prevent the Asian Pacific from falling under the economic domination of Japan; Japan might rearm, perhaps with nuclear weapons, precipitating a huge arms race in the region; a military confrontation with Japan could not be excluded. The scope of these negative implications provides ample incentive for both Washington and Tokyo to place their relationship near the top of their respective foreign policy agendas.

As of late 1995, most American analysts were not unduly pessimistic about U.S.-Japan ties, although some saw imminent changes in the nature of the relationship. Chalmers Johnson, for example, argued that the U.S. security treaty with Japan should be rewritten to enable the United States to continue to provide nuclear and strategic stability for Asia, but to force Japan to shift to a consumer driven economy. Johnson said there was little use for American ground troops in Japan and Korea after the Cold War, although the United States should maintain its ability to project power into the region. In his view, a withdrawal of American ground forces would not cause instability. Indeed, Asian stability had come about, not because of the U.S. military presence in Asia, but because of the region's dynamic economic growth.[25]

An opposing view was presented by Ezra Vogel, who argued the U.S.-Japan security treaty should be preserved because it helped to maintain regional stability. However, the treaty should be adapted to new missions due to uncertainty over North Korean and Chinese policies. An advocate of forward deployed U.S. ground troops in Asia, Vogel noted that in 1995 only about 3 percent of the total U.S. defense budget of $250 billion went to U.S. forces in the Pacific, an extremely low cost to American taxpayers given Asia's growing importance to the United States.[26]

The greatest restraints on Japan once again becoming an enemy of the United States might be self-generated. In the postwar period, the Japanese people have not favored the rebuilding of a power projection capability, and one legacy of brutal policies during the Second World War has been continued mistrust of Japan by its neighbors. Under present conditions, Japan does not have the moral authority to lead the region. Indeed, most Asian countries, including China, see value in a continued U.S. military presence in Japan as insurance against the possibility that Tokyo might one day embark on a new program of rearmament and expansion.

Collective Security and Multilateralism

One strategy effectively utilized by the United States in the postwar period has been to mold the international system to serve American security, political, economic, and ideological interests. Rejecting world domination as an appropriate strategy after World War II, the United States used its global influence to help establish international institutions such as the United Nations, World Bank, and International Monetary Fund. For the most part, this was done in cooperation with countries sharing U.S. interests in a peaceful, stable, and prosperous world. As the communist threat coalesced, the United States helped to organize collective security arrangements such as the North Atlantic Treaty Organization (NATO), Southeast Asia Treaty Organization (SEATO), Central Treaty Organization (CENTO), and the Australia-New Zealand-United States Treaty (ANZUS).

Unlike Europe, where NATO performed quite well, collective security in Asia was not too effective. SEATO was abandoned after the Vietnam War; and the United States came to rely more heavily on bilateral security treaties and arrangements negotiated with Japan, South Korea, the Republic of China (until 1979), the Philippines, Thailand, and Australia.

The United States emphasized bilateral rather than multilateral security arrangements in Asia for three principal reasons. First, Asia's security environment was different from that of Europe. Historical animosities and the lack of a common enemy worked against collective security in Asia, making it easier for Washington to manage security issues on a bilateral basis. In most cases, U.S. relations with Asian nations were better than relations between Asian states themselves. Second, the United States avoided regional security arrangements in Asia because such arrangements were suggested by Moscow. The USSR repeatedly proposed that it join Washington in multilateral discussions of Asian security issues. Washington saw these proposals as Soviet ploys to gain a political foothold in Asia and rejected the suggestions. Third, the United States possessed the most powerful military force in the Western Pacific. It did not require a coalition of Asian nations to protect vital American interests, most of which were maritime in nature and well within U.S. capabilities to defend.

In the late 1980s, as Soviet President Mikhail Gorbachev reduced Moscow's military presence overseas, the regional balance of power in Asia changed significantly. The United States became the sole superpower, but it was apparent that American forces, too, would soon be reduced in Asia. Soviet and American military reductions were accompanied by Chinese efforts to modernize the PLA and to increase its power projection capabilities. By 1991 discussions were common in Asia over how regional security arrangements might replace the American defense umbrella.

Addressing these concerns, Secretary of State James Baker urged Asian countries to move cautiously before creating new alliances to replace those that were "tried and tested frameworks" with the United States. Baker said, "We have had a remarkable degree of stability in this region....We ought to be careful about changing those arrangements and discarding them for something else unless we're absolutely certain that the something else is better and will work."[27]

Meanwhile, some American scholars concluded that changing circumstances justified a new look at collective security in Asia. The Brookings Institution published a study of American defense needs in the post-Cold War era which recommended the adoption of a strategy of "cooperative engagement."[28] The study estimated the United States could reduce its defense spending by one-third over the next ten years and still maintain the world's preeminent military establishment, capable of dealing with any emergency, if it relied more on collective security arrangements. The study proposed the United States seek to engage potential adversaries and competitors in cooperative security ventures to minimize the risk of future military conflict, in much the same way that Washington had used cooperative engagement to coopt the German and Japanese military establishments following World War II. The study argued, "The future ability of the United States to maintain the conditions of its security will depend as much on its moral authority, diplomatic skills, and economic assets as on its military capabilities."

By late 1991 the Bush administration also began to place greater emphasis on Asian collective security. Baker suggested the United States, China, Japan, and the Soviet Union work together in joint action to prevent nuclear proliferation on the Korean peninsula, the "number-one threat to security in Northeast Asia."[29] A similar cooperative policy on Cambodia was adopted through the sponsorship of the U.N. Security Council.

Asian support for collective security grew during 1992. Singapore's Foreign Minister Wong Kan Seng told the Asia Society in New York that a tripartite pact including the United States, China, and Japan should be formed to replace the weakening U.S. strategic presence in Southeast Asia.[30] After Clinton assumed office in January 1993, his administration supported multilateral discussions on regional security in Asia by participating in the ASEAN Regional Forum and proposing a Northeast Asian security dialogue.

Any strategy based on collective security in Asia faces considerable obstacles. Two of the most important are the region's great diversity and lack of a common threat. This raises questions about the purpose of collective security in Asia: Against whom is the arrangement intended? And if no threat is identified, why create a collective security arrangement in the first place?

These questions have special relevance because of China. Although most Asian nations are worried about the modernization of the PLA and the possibility of Chinese hegemony, few governments identify China as a direct threat and none wants to exclude the PRC from regional security discussions. Due to Chinese sensitivity, security issues in the South China Sea are difficult to address in these forums. There is also the matter of Taiwan. Whenever China participates, it generally demands that Taiwan be excluded. In view of these constraints, most Asian governments consider collective security not as an instrument to defend against a common enemy or a forum to discuss specific security issues, but rather as a useful political and psychological device to restrain ambitious countries like China through personal interaction and the preservation of national face.

A strategy of collective security in Asia is an option for the United States, but one which might not be sufficient to protect the full range of American interests in the region. U.S. collective security strategies could take many forms, depending upon variables such as the degree of U.S. leadership; the level of American participation; the membership, structure, and responsibility of the collective security organization; and the types of security issues to be addressed by the organization.

Collective security can be seen as part of broader multilateral strategy to serve U.S. interests in Asia. Again, there are numerous forms a multilateral strategy could take, with one key variable being the level of U.S. leadership and participation. For example, a multilateral strategy could be based on an active U.S. leadership role in which Washington would seek to control regional organizations. Or, a multilateral strategy could be based on the United States playing a more supportive role and working through consensus with other Pacific Rim countries to define and achieve mutual goals.

A strong U.S. leadership role was advocated by former Secretary of Defense Robert S. McNamara.[31] Arguing that it was the historic opportunity and responsibility of the United States to develop a vision for the new world order, McNamara proposed a collective security system based on the rule of law among nations. The United States should retain the military means to fight and win wars, but the essential U.S. role should be to lead other Western democracies in the establishment of a new world order. McNamara's strategy was similar to those based on the view that the United States had a moral mission to lead the Asian Pacific toward a more enlightened, democratic, and free market future: a new Pacific community.

One advocate of a more supportive role for the United States in a multilateral strategy was George McGhee, former undersecretary of state for political affairs during the Kennedy administration. He recommended the United States adopt a "strategy of unilateral restraint" to replace the balance of power mentality that dominated the Cold War.[32]   Such a strategy would not result in American disengagement from the world, but rather increased global cooperation.

> Through confederations, treaties, bilateral and multilateral pacts and private arrangements, the international community is constantly expanding. It is binding democratic nations and peoples together, inexorably producing not only a barrier to war but also greater cooperation in dealing with the severe global problems of pollution, poverty and other social ills. This progress represents the ultimate concept of an effective new world system.

McGhee pointed to the United Nations, NATO, the Conference on Security and Cooperation in Europe, and regional trading agreements as examples of international organizations that have replaced the need for unilateral intervention by the United States.   Applying this strategy to Asia, the United States would help create multinational organizations to substitute for American predominance in political, economic, and security affairs.   If such organizations could be established, Asian-Pacific countries could reduce their armed forces and still enjoy the benefits of security and stability.   McGhee was confident that U.S. intelligence would give ample warning to prepare the nation for any future confrontation, although enemies were difficult to identify at this stage of history.

Other multilateral strategies rely heavily on the United Nations.   The U.N. Transitional Authority in Cambodia (UNTAC), which played a major role in bringing peace to Cambodia from 1991-1993, is pointed to as an example of U.S. interests being served through the U.N.   Under this strategy, similar to the "assertive multilateralism" of the Clinton administration, the United States would assist the United Nations to settle regional crises without unilaterally committing American forces.

One advantage of multilateral strategies is that they reflect current trends toward wider cooperation in international politics.   Most Asian nations seem willing to work with the United States in international organizations to help solve regional problems, but most governments demand an equal voice in deciding what to do.   Under strategies of collective security and multilateralism, the United States would depend on the United Nations and multilateral organizations in Asia to provide both the forum for discussion of regional issues and the authorization for collective action if needed.

Isolationism

One enduring characteristic of U.S. foreign policy is a tendency toward isolationism. A very limited constituency exists in the United States for costly overseas involvement, as discovered by every administration as it attempts to persuade Congress to appropriate foreign aid.

The strength of isolationism in the United States is such that foreign leaders feel compelled to urge the American people to remain engaged in world affairs. German Chancellor Helmut Kohl appealed to the U.S. public to consider that "the destiny of the world is being decided on the foreign policy front and that each people that does not understand and follow this lesson of history will pay very dearly for it....For a people such as the American people, whether it wants it or not, that has a decisive role to play in world politics and will have to play this role, this is even more valid."[33] These sentiments were echoed by former British Prime Minister Margaret Thatcher, who urged the United States repeatedly during the Reagan and Bush administrations not to abandon America's leadership role in world affairs. On another occasion, South Korean President Roh Tae Woo told President Bush that without the presence of the United States in Asia, "it is bad news for all of us."[34]

Nonetheless, American isolationists could well ask a number of difficult questions regarding U.S. interests in Asia:

1. Why should the United States be involved in maintaining a balance of power in Asia when Asian nations are capable of defining and sustaining such a balance themselves?
2. Why should the American people bear the burden of maintaining a strong military presence in the Asian Pacific, when Asian security should be a matter for Asian nations to preserve?
3. Where in Asia is there a threat to American interests that justifies a large forward based military presence, when not even a nuclear-armed North Korea threatens the vital interests of the United States?
4. What damage to vital American interests would occur if the United States reduced its leadership role and military presence in the Pacific?

American isolationism crosses party lines, and it is not a conservative or liberal issue. William Hyland argued in 1991 that the United States should downgrade the importance of foreign policy and national security and concentrate instead on rebuilding America.[35] What America needed, he said, was "a psychological turn inward," despite the toll on American foreign policy.

Hyland believed the United States should not take on new commitments or even maintain most of the ones created during the Cold War. The American people would not support intervention around the world on moral grounds or pay $200-$300 billion annually for defense to counter "instability." He recommended the United States avoid new entanglements abroad, withdraw the bulk of its armed forces from overseas, and cut back drastically on foreign aid. The United States had to learn to trust the Germans and the Japanese, he said, and to leave only a skeletal framework of military forces for emergency deployment.

A similar argument was presented in a 1992 report from the Carnegie Endowment for International Peace.[36] The report recommended:

1. U.S. foreign policy must be built on renewed domestic strength. Rebuilding the U.S. economy should be the nation's number one priority, but not through protectionism or purely regional trade organizations at the expense of international free trade and competition.
2. U.S. leadership in the world must continue, but with a new emphasis on collective action in support of peace, democracy, and open trade.
3. Germany and Japan should become permanent members of the U.N. Security Council, acknowledging their preeminent role in economic and political affairs while also having them contribute more to international operations.
4. The United States should withdraw military forces deployed abroad while strengthening the peacekeeping functions of the United Nations.

Randall Forsberg argued that the United States no longer needed $100 billion of its annual $240 billion defense budget, since the Pentagon's strategy for fighting two simultaneous major regional conflicts was unrealistic.[37] Major portions of the defense budget, he said, should be diverted to domestic programs such as education, cancer research, infrastructure improvement, and affordable housing. Forsberg proposed a strategy of "cooperative security" based on mutual arms reductions and multilateral peacekeeping. The system would be based on the principles of nonviolent conflict resolution and nonoffensive defense. Under cooperative security the United States would work with Russia and China to reduce ground, air, and naval weapons systems built during the Cold War, negotiate a moratorium on new production of these systems, and negotiate a moratorium on major arms exports.

These neo-isolationist views are reminders that two of the most persistent debates in U.S. foreign policy are internationalism versus isolationism and multilateralism versus unilateralism. As Michael Mandelbaum described the foreign policy debates in Congress in mid-1995: "The Democrats tend toward multilateralism, but also blame the U.N. for its own failures in Somalia. The GOP strives for unilateralism, but through budget-cutting, reduces America's global reach."[38]

There also is fundamental disagreement over how American "leadership" and "capabilities" should be employed in foreign policy. In early 1995 Senate majority leader Bob Dole stressed American "leadership" in a unilateral approach in which Clinton's concepts of assertive multilateralism and enlargement were discarded in favor of hardheaded analysis of what is truly in the national interest.[39] At the time, the Republican-led Congress was seeking to limit the use of American military forces to situations where U.S. security interests were directly threatened, as opposed to lending American military support to multilateral operations where U.S. security interests were seen to be more marginal.

The essential characteristic of isolationist strategies toward Asia is the expectation that Asian-Pacific countries will take care of themselves. They do not need the United States as their shepherd, nor can the United States afford to play such a role in a period of budget constraints and competing domestic priorities. "America-first" strategies generally do not envision the abandonment of U.S. interests in Asia, but rather a redefinition of those interests to ensure that American resources are not wasted in overseas activities than can be handled by others.

Integration

A quite different approach from isolationism is a strategy of integration. Proponents of this strategy -- including the author -- think that U.S. interests are best served by leading efforts toward greater interdependence and cooperation in the Pacific Basin.[40]

Integration became an important U.S. objective under President Bush, who equated the challenges of integration with those of containment:

The grand strategy of the West during the postwar period has been based on the concept of containment: checking the Soviet Union's expansionist aims, in the hope that the Soviet system itself would one day be forced to confront its internal contradictions. The ferment in the Soviet Union today affirms the wisdom of this strategy. And now we have a precious opportunity to move beyond containment....

Our goal -- integrating the Soviet Union into the community of nations -- is every bit as ambitious as containment was at its time. And it holds tremendous promise for international stability.[41]

Under a strategy of integration as proposed by the author, President Bush's goal of integrating Moscow into the international community for the purpose of speeding its transition to a market democracy would be applied to countries such as China, North Korea, Vietnam, Cambodia, Laos, and Burma. It is assumed that constructive engagement with these countries would be more effective in bringing about long-term change in their political and economic systems than isolating their governments from the world community.

Thus, the first priority of this strategy is to integrate nonmarket Asian economies into regional economic and political systems, which largely reflect principles of the free market and political pluralism, in order to stabilize the international system in Asia and contribute to regional peace and prosperity. There is evidence that integration may help to achieve these goals. A correlation seems to exist between efforts by authoritarian states to join global economic and political systems and the setting aside of intentions to destroy those systems. Communist countries seeking to integrate with the world community, for example, cooperated in trying to find peaceful solutions to issues such as Afghanistan, Cambodia, the reunification of Germany, the Persian Gulf crisis, and divisions on the Korean peninsula. By late 1995, all socialist governments in Asia -- with the possible exception of Pyongyang -- had expressed keen interest in becoming part of regional and subregional communities.

A strategy of integration also has an important economic dimension, referred to by Assistant Secretary of State Richard Solomon as "integration in economics."[42] The Bush and Clinton administrations strongly supported economic integration in the Asia-Pacific region because of growing U.S. interdependence with other Pacific Rim economies. U.S. encouragement of APEC demonstrated Washington's commitment to this process of integration.

A third dimension of integration strategy involves security. The movement toward discussion of security issues in various Asian-Pacific forums epitomizes this type of integration. Security integration in Asia was not well developed during the Bush administration, but President Clinton advanced this goal through U.S. support for regional security dialogues in the ASEAN Regional Forum (ARF) and proposals for security consultations in Northeast Asia.

A strategy of integration envisioned by the author would depend heavily on U.S. forward deployed forces in the Western Pacific. These are necessary for several reasons: the post-Cold War era is a time of uncertainty and instability in some Asian countries; Russian nuclear and conventional forces remain in Northeast Asia; several new threats to U.S. interests are emerging; and the U.S. military presence reduces incentives for regional arms races, encourages Asian governments to seek peaceful resolution of disputes, and supports U.S. leadership in the region.

A fourth dimension of a strategy of integration is political. To date, very little has been accomplished in the area of political integration in Asia, and progress ought to be slow. All Asian-Pacific countries value their political independence and jealously guard their status as sovereign states. Nonetheless, useful steps toward regional political cooperation have been taken in multilateral discussions of noneconomic issues in the annual APEC summit meetings initiated by President Clinton in Seattle in 1993. Political integration is not necessary for other dimensions of integration to proceed.

A U.S. strategy of integration in Asia might have four fundamental objectives:

1. to maintain regional security and deterrence at both nuclear and conventional levels at lower cost to the American taxpayer
2. to expedite the integration of Asian socialist countries into regional economic and political systems, thus reducing regional threats and enhancing peace and stability
3. to enable the United States to continue its leadership role in the Pacific Basin
4. to influence the evolving Asia-Pacific international order in ways supportive of U.S. goals, interests, and objectives.

Such a strategy would not seek the elimination of national boundaries, state sovereignty, or cultural diversity in Asia. The process of integration would be flexible in its timetable and framework. No country would be forced into an unwanted role or relationship. Through consultation and cooperation, integration would broaden the range of mutual interests. The fundamental purpose of integration would be to serve these mutual interests by contributing to national prosperity and regional peace.

One of the strengths of a strategy of integration is congruity with trends of regional interdependence. There is widespread recognition in the Asian Pacific of the need for increased cooperation between regional governments on a broad range of issues. Integration builds on interdependency and counters trends toward disintegration and fragmentation, which often can be found in small and lesser developed countries seeking to build "new institutions of identity, sovereignty, and legitimacy."[43] Both trends exist in today's world, but integration strengthens the international system while disintegration tears it apart.

A more limited integration strategy, focused almost exclusively on economic cooperation, can be found in the APEC process. The advisory Eminent Persons Group (EPG) recommended to Asian-Pacific ministers in 1994 "the progressive development of a community of Asia Pacific economies with free and open trade and investment."[44] According to the EPG, "community" was not meant to imply full economic integration or even a customs union, but "simply to connote a like-minded group that aims to remove barriers to economic exchange among its members in the interests of all." The community would be based on several principles, including free trade and investment, international cooperation, regional solidarity, mutual benefit, mutual respect, egalitarianism, pragmatism, decisionmaking on the basis of consensus, implementation on the basis of flexibility, and "open regionalism." The EPG did not recommend an Asian-Pacific free trade area, but rather free trade in the broadest sense of the word.

The APEC process was driven primarily by business and trade. In 1994 the Pacific Business Forum recommended that APEC adopt a framework for free trade and investment and investment liberalization and investment initiatives.[45] Other recommendations included business facilitation, transparency of regulations, ease of border restrictions, harmonizing of domestic product standards, implementation of intellectual property rights, harmonizing regulations on technology transfer, establishment of mechanisms to settle disputes, and adoption of good business ethics. In addition, the Forum advocated more intensive efforts to develop human resources and the adoption of business development policies, including cultural exchanges, support to small and medium enterprises, and infrastructure development. Improvement in government and business partnership and business networking were also suggested by the advisory group.

The APEC vision was based on the belief that all members "had a deep interest in developing a community of Asia Pacific economies and could reap large additional gains from trade through further liberalization in the region." The difficulties of building such an economic community were considerable: great diversity in cultures, languages, legal systems, levels of economic development, and degree of implementation of market principles; protectionist pressures; inward-looking regionalism; and the possibility that some members might disengage. But beyond these difficulties, all APEC participants saw potential advantage in greater regional economic cooperation. APEC thus represented an integrative strategy based on economics that was limited in scope and pragmatic in policy, but also optimistic and visionary. As described by the Eminent Persons Group: "We are pursuing the first truly intercontinental economic enterprise."

The limits of integration through APEC were at least temporarily reached in November 1995, when Secretary of Defense William Perry suggested to the Nihon Keizai Shimbun newspaper, "It's possible to expand APEC to an organization that can take up security problems. This could act as a foundation for building mutual confidence in Asia." Japan's Prime Minister Tomiichi Murayama said he did not object to discussing security questions in APEC, but most other APEC leaders attending the Osaka, Japan meeting insisted that APEC be confined to economic discussions and that the ASEAN Regional Forum (ARF) be used to discuss security issues. [46]

Security integration through ARF also had its limits. Under ASEAN's sponsorship, ARF annually brought foreign ministers together to discuss regional security issues. Controversy generally was avoided, however, including discussion of issues such as the high level of military spending in the region, disputes in the South China Sea, the Korean peninsula, the China-Taiwan military confrontation, China's rapid military buildup, and the lucrative weapons trade in the region. Nonetheless, face-to-face multilateral dialogue on security issues was thought to contribute to confidence-building in the region.

The processes of integration are underway in the Asian Pacific; but unless the United States exercises decisive leadership, it may be unable to take advantage of integration. In November 1995, for example, President Clinton decided at the last minute not to attend the APEC leaders' meeting in Osaka due to budget disputes with Congress. His absence caused many Asians to comment that the United States was losing its credibility in the region. Instead of the United States demonstrating leadership at the meeting, PRC President Jiang Zemin became the outstanding statesman when he announced that China would slash its overall tariffs by an average of 30 percent on more than 4,000 tariff lines beginning in 1996.[47]

Many of the forces of integration come from within Asia itself. In 1994 48.5 percent of Asia's exports were to other Asian countries, up from about 42 percent in 1990. Japan's two-way trade with Asia grew 40 percent during 1990-1994, while its trade with the European Union dropped 19 percent and trade with the United States fell 5 percent. China likewise became a major engine of Asian economic growth, purchasing nearly 6 percent of Asia's total exports in 1994, double its share in 1990.[48]

In another demonstration of Asian integration excluding the United States, the Association of Southeast Asian Nations -- the preeminent example of integration at the subregional level -- pledged in December 1995 to speed up the elimination of tariffs within ASEAN. Most will be eliminated by the year 2003, with tariffs cut to between zero and 5 percent by the year 2000 on many items. ASEAN also agreed to liberalize trade in services and to establish a regional patent and trademark system.[49]

Also in December 1995, the ten nations of Southeast Asia adopted the Treaty on Southeast Asian Nuclear Weapon-Free Zone (SEANWFZ), declaring the region nuclear free and asking the world's nuclear powers to honor the ban. China joined the United States in opposing certain sections of the treaty: Beijing because the treaty impinged on some of China's territorial claims in the Spratlys, and Washington because SEANWFZ threatened some bilateral security treaties with Asian countries and inhibited the movement of American nuclear-armed and nuclear-powered warships through the region.[50]

Another sign of growing independence from the United States is the rediscovery of Asian heritage. The "American way" seems to be losing some of its appeal while the "Asian way" seems to be taking firmer root.[51] While the term is not clearly defined and the evidence anecdotal, the growing popularity of the "Asian way" reflects a heightened sense of pride and accomplishment within Asia. At the same time, there is growing criticism of the American way of life for being too free and prone to social catastrophe. Many Asian leaders have commented on this phenomenon.

Thus, the forces of integration in the Asian Pacific, while powerful and of possible utility to the United States, must be studied and understood. Effective U.S. leadership is essential if Washington is to remain on top of the process. Strategies of integration vary considerably in terms of their dimensions -- economic, security, political, or cultural -- and in terms of organization, e.g., the extent to which integration is institutionalized, and whether decisions are made by consensus or dominant power. All integrative strategies are based on the assumption that wider cooperation between nation-states will improve the international system while protecting the self-interest of individual countries. The creation of a supernational body to manage Asian-Pacific affairs is not an objective of integration.

Conclusion

Most of the strategic options reviewed in this chapter can be grouped around major themes in U.S. strategy toward the Asian Pacific: deterrence, balance of power, countering emerging threats, collective security, multilateralism, tendencies toward isolationism, and integration.

The strategy of convergent deterrence suggested that the U.S. security infrastructure built in the Asia-Pacific during the Cold War could be used in new ways. Instead of deterring the global Soviet threat, convergent deterrence focused on a regional mission of preserving the peace through a combination of deterrence and greater cooperation with U.S. friends and allies.

Balance of power strategies sought to position the United States in a favorable geopolitical relationship with Japan, China, and Russia, the three nations most likely to challenge U.S. power in the Western Pacific in the next century. One approach was to counterbalance growing Chinese power through a closer alliance with Japan. At the same time, the U.S. military presence in Japan would prevent the reemergence of a new threat from Tokyo.

Another balance of power approach suggested closer U.S. cooperation with both Japan and China. A constructive triangular relationship would discourage these nations -- as well as Russia -- from pursuing hegemony and building up their military forces to levels threatening the United States.

Other approaches viewed the strategic quadrangle of the United States, Japan, China, and Russia as determining the future of the Asian Pacific. Of these relationships, the most critical in maintaining a balance of power in Asia would be U.S.-Japan-China triangular relations. The

U.S. relationship with Tokyo was the key strategic alliance, but that alliance would be impossible to maintain if U.S.-China relations were severely confrontational.

Another balance of power strategy proposed that the United States keep its distance from both Japan and China. Instead, the United States should rely heavily on Russia to ensure that neither Asian country became too powerful.

Various strategies could be constructed under the assumption that China or Japan will become the most powerful threat to U.S. interests in Asia over the next several decades. These strategies included containment through unilateral U.S. action or collective security; retrenchment from Asia to avoid conflict with either power; accommodation of Chinese and Japanese ambitions; carrot-and-stick approaches to manipulate Beijing and Tokyo in directions favoring U.S. interests; neutralizing the threats by entering into an alliance or close partnership with the challenging country; using international organizations to restrain hegemonic intentions; and deliberately drawing China or Japan into a war with the United States to defeat the Asian power before it became too strong.

Other strategies sought to revitalize the U.S.-Japan security alliance. Some strategies suggested the U.S.-Japan security treaty be revised; some recommended it be discarded; still others believed the treaty could be adapted to meet new challenges such as uncertainties over North Korea and China.

There was a wide range of strategic options based on collective security and multilateralism. One key variable was the level of U.S. leadership and participation in multilateral organizations. Other variables included whether the objective be dialogue or more formal arrangements; whether the agenda be limited, specific, or broad; whether the organization be pro forma or an effective instrument of action; whether the focus of collective security be against a national threat, a regional threat such as proliferation, or left deliberately vague; and whether the membership be inclusive or exclusive.

Strategies tending toward isolationism sought to limit U.S. involvement in the Asian Pacific to those circumstances where direct U.S. interests were at stake. Emphasis was placed on American domestic issues, allowing Asian-Pacific countries to solve most of their own problems.

Strategies of integration had several objectives, including the involvement of nonmarket countries into mainstream Asian-Pacific affairs, closer economic cooperation, wider security consultations, and more frequent high-level discussions between political leaders. Integration strategies attempted to merge U.S. policy in the Pacific with trends toward interdependence, while at the same time to preserve U.S. leadership in security, political, economic, and cultural dimensions. To date, the most effective strategy confined integration to matters of free and open trade and investment, such as the APEC process. As reflected in ASEAN and SEANWFZ, integration in Asia was not dependent on U.S. leadership or active participation.

Notes

1. William T. Tow, *Encountering the Dominant Player: U.S. Extended Deterrence Strategy in the Asia-Pacific* (New York: Columbia University Press, 1991).

2. See, for example, Nixon's comments in *Wall Street Journal*, June 1, 1993, p. A12.

3. See Henry Kissinger, "Why We Can't Withdraw From Asia," *Washington Post*, June 15, 1993, p. A21. An interesting discussion of the difficulty in balancing realism and idealism in American foreign policy can be found in his *Diplomacy* (New York: Simon & Schuster, 1994).

4. Henry Kissinger, "Heading for a Collision in Asia," *Washington Post*, July 26, 1995, p. A23.

5. See Kissinger's interview in *Far Eastern Economic Review*, November 16, 1995, pp. 26-30.

6. Richard H. Solomon, "Who Will Shape the Emerging Structure of East Asia?" in Michael Mandelbaum, ed., *The Strategic Quadrangle: Russia, China, Japan, and the United States in East Asia* (New York: Council on Foreign Relations, 1994), pp. 196-208.

7. Michael Lind, "Asia First: A Foreign Policy," *New York Times*, April 18, 1995, p. A25.

8. A summary of these acquisitions can be found in *National Security: Impact of China's Military Modernization in the Pacific Region* (Washington, D.C.: U.S. General Accounting Office, June 1995), pp. 16-27. See also, John Caldwell, *China's Conventional Military Capabilities, 1994-2004* (Washington, D.C.: Center for Strategic and International Studies, 1994); and Michael D. Swaine, "The Modernization of the Chinese People's Liberation Army: Prospects and Implications for Northeast Asia," *NPR Analysis*, Vol. 5, No. 3 (October 1994).

9. B.A. Hamzah, "China's Strategy," *Far Eastern Economic Review*, August 13, 1992, p. 22.

10. One Southeast Asian diplomat stationed in Beijing said in July 1995: "Since the end of the Cold War, China has become the undisputed regional power here, but its Spratly Island claims and its threats against Taiwan are causing growing unease." United Press International report from Beijing, July 20, 1995.

11. Nayan Chanda and Kari Huss, "China: The New Nationalism," *Far Eastern Economic Review*, November 9, 1995, pp. 20-28.

12. Reuters report from Beijing, December 11, 1995.

13. Xinhua reported in December 1995 that a group of twenty-five generals and officers from the PLA's National Defense University held a meeting in which they said some Western nations (not identified, but clearly meaning the United States) were "motivated by their concerns of global strategic interests" to "contain China and stop its development." Associated Press report from Beijing, December 17, 1995. The extent to which these concerns are genuine is unknown. Chinese psychological efforts to manipulate the American government into greater concessions over issues such as Taiwan are well documented. See, for example, Lucian W. Pye, *Chinese Commercial Negotiating Style* (Cambridge, MA: Oelgeschlager, Gunn and Haig Publishers, 1982); and Richard H. Solomon, *Chinese Political Negotiating Behavior: A Briefing Analysis* (Santa Monica: Rand Corporation, 1985). See also Nicholas Eftimiades, *Chinese Intelligence Operations* (Annapolis: Naval Institute Press, 1994).

14. For a summary of the report, carried by the New China News Agency (Xinhua), see *China News*, August 17, 1992, p. 1.

15. USCINCPAC Admiral Richard C. Macke's statements on the escalating tension between the Philippines and China over disputed Spratly islands were illustrative: "I am concerned with the actions of several countries that have increased the tension level in the South China Sea....I have no indications from diplomatic, intelligence or any other sources that [Chinese leaders] are contemplating any military action in the South China Sea." Reuters report from Manila, June 15, 1995; United Press International report from Manila, June 15, 1995. Elsewhere he said: "If we confront China and try to isolate China we are guaranteeing an outcome. If we keep working with them there's a possibility that they will come into the Asia-Pacific as a contributing member to the stability that exists." Reuters report from Townsville, Australia, August 15, 1995.

16. In 1994 the United States registered its largest trade imbalance since 1988, at $108.1 billion. The largest bilateral deficits were $65.7 billion with Japan, followed by $25.5 billion with China. The Japanese surplus grew 11 percent over 1993, while the Chinese surplus grew 30 percent. U.S. Commerce Department figures cited in *Washington Post*, February 18, 1995, p. D1.

17. United Press International report from Beijing, October 28, 1994.

18. *Far Eastern Economic Review*, November 9, 1995, p. 26.

19. See Dennis Van Vranken Hickey, *United States-Taiwan Security Ties: From Cold War to Beyond Containment* (Westport, CT: Praeger, 1994), pp. 79-81.

20. Chinese military leaders asked Assistant Secretary of Defense Joseph Nye during his December 1995 trip to Beijing how the United States would react to a military crisis over Taiwan. Nye said he responded: "Nobody knows." Citing the U.S. decision to go to war in Korea in 1950, he commented, "It shows that you cannot know the answer to these things." Nye said the dangers of escalation in the Taiwan Strait "could be catastrophic." Reuters report from Washington, D.C., December 12, 1995.

21. John McCain, "Let's Normalize Relations with Vietnam," *Washington Post*, May 21, 1995, p. C7.

22. *New York Times*, November 12, 1991, p. A1.

23. The formal U.S. effort to expand the U.N. Security Council to include both Japan and Germany as permanent members began in June 1993.

24. Figures for Japan and China taken from *The Military Balance: 1994-1995* (London: International Institute for Strategic Studies, 1994), pp. 170, 176.

25. See "Uncertain Future: Is the U.S.-Japan Alliance Past Its Prime?" *Far Eastern Economic Review*, November 23, 1995, pp. 20-22.

26. Ibid.

27. *New York Times*, July 25, 1991, p. A14.

28. William W. Kaufmann and John D. Steinbruner, *Decisions for Defense: Prospects for a New Order* (Washington, D.C.: The Brookings Institution, 1991).

29. *Washington Post*, November 11, 1991, p. A21.

30. *China News*, October 19, 1992, p. 7.

31. See *New York Times*, February 3, 1992, p. A8.

32. George C. McGhee, "`Balance of Restraint' in an Unsettled World," *Washington Post*, April 12, 1992, p. C4.

33. *Washington Post*, March 23, 1992, p. A10.

34. *New York Times*, January 7, 1992, p. A8.

35. William G. Hyland, "Downgrade Foreign Policy," *New York Times*, May 20, 1991, p. A15.

36. National Commission on America and the New World, *Changing Our Ways: America and the New World* (Washington, D.C.: Carnegie Endowment for International Peace, 1992).

37. See Randall Forsberg, "Wasting Billions," *Boston Review*, Vol. 19, No. 2 (April-May 1994); and "Creating a Cooperative Security System," ibid., Vol. 17, No. 6 (November-December 1992).

38. Quoted in *Washington Post*, May 1, 1995, p. A4.

39. For reports on this modern isolationism versus internationalism debate, see *Washington Post*, March 2, 1995, p. A1; ibid., March 3, 1995, p. A25.

40. Martin L. Lasater, "Beyond Containment in Asia: An American Strategy for the 1990s," *Korean Journal of Defense Analysis*, Vol. 3, No. 2 (Winter 1991), pp. 83-104.

41. George Bush, "Security Strategy for the 1990s," *Department of State Current Policy*, No. 1178 (May 1989), p. 2.

42. Richard H. Solomon, "Asian Security in the 1990s: Integration in Economics, Diversity in Defense," *Department of State Dispatch*, Vol. 1, No. 10 (November 5, 1990).

43. I. William Zartman, review of *Beyond the Cold War: New Dimensions in International Relations*, edited by Geir Lundestad and Odd Arne Westad (New York: Oxford University Press, 1993), in *American Political Science Review*, Vol. 89, No. 1 (March 1995), p. 257.

44. See the Second Report of the Eminent Persons Group, *Achieving the APEC Vision: Free and Open Trade in the Asia Pacific* (Singapore: Asia-Pacific Economic Cooperation Secretariat, August 1994).

45. Report of the Pacific Business Forum, *A Business Blueprint for APEC: Strategies for Growth and Common Prosperity* (Singapore: Asia-Pacific Economic Cooperation Secretariat, October 1994).

46. Reuters reports from Osaka, Japan, November 15, 1995, and November 19, 1995; also Associated Press report from Osaka on November 19, 1995.

47. *Washington Post*, November 24, 1995, p. F3.

48. *Wall Street Journal*, November 17, 1995, p. A13A.

49. *Wall Street Journal*, December 18, 1995, p. A11.

50. *Washington Post*, December 16, 1995, p. A28.

51. See *Washington Post*, November 19, 1995, p. C2.

6

Conclusion

The preceding chapters outlined a wide range of strategic options toward Asia available to the United States through the end of this century. This final chapter will summarize the strategies discussed and make several recommendations.

Summary

Under President Bush, the United States moved beyond containment to a new global strategy of building a community of market democracies. Collective engagement and integration became major themes, as efforts were made to define U.S. strategy not only in security terms but also in economic, political, and cultural terms. The Bush administration changed U.S. military strategy from being prepared to fight a global war against the Soviet Union to being prepared to fight two simultaneous regional contingencies, one of which was always a second Korean War scenario. The base force to carry out this mission required substantially fewer military resources than those needed during the Cold War.

To replace containment in Asia, the Bush administration adopted a strategy of building a new partnership in the Pacific with closer, more equal, and more comprehensive ties being established with traditional allies like Japan. New levels of cooperation were established with all countries in the region, even nations formerly hostile to the United States. The emphasis was on integration rather than exclusion, with far greater attention being paid to the economic aspects of U.S. strategy toward the region. At the same time, the United States became seriously concerned over regional (especially Chinese and North Korean) proliferation of weapons of mass destruction and advanced means of delivery such as missiles. In adjusting to the new security environment in Asia, the Pentagon began the East Asia strategic initiative (EASI) process that broaden the role of U.S. forward deployed forces at the same time they were being reduced by about 25 percent through 1995. The Bush administration described the U.S. role in the Asian Pacific as "regional balancer, honest broker, and ultimate security guarantor."

The process of redefining U.S. global and regional strategy continued under the Clinton administration, which adopted most aspects of Bush strategy. On the global level, President Clinton implemented a national security strategy of engagement and enlargement with the primary goal to expand and strengthen the community of market democracies. The three pillars of the strategy -- economic growth, military strength, and support for democracy -- were given equal priority, making it sometimes difficult to avoid contradictions in policy. For a time, assertive multilateralism was in vogue, but frustration with U.N.-directed efforts in Somalia and Bosnia proved that multinational efforts could not substitute for U.S. leadership and decisive unilateral action.

Militarily, the Clinton administration conducted a bottom-up review that resulted in additional cuts in U.S. armed forces but that continued the Bush strategy of being able to win two major regional conflicts occurring nearly simultaneously. Once again, North Korea played prominently in contingency planning. As viewed by the Pentagon, the U.S. grand strategy was engagement, prevention, and partnership, with heavy emphasis on building a coalition of democracies. The administration insisted it would use American forces unilaterally, in alliance or partnership, or multilaterally solely on the basis of what best served U.S. interests in any given situation.

Regionally, the Clinton administration pursued a grand strategy of building a new Pacific community. The five building blocks of the integrated strategy included a reinvigorated U.S.-Japan global partnership; promotion of more open economies and greater trade; active support for democracy; firm American commitments to its military alliances; and forward U.S. presence in Japan, South Korea, and throughout the Asian-Pacific region. Equal priority was given to economic, security, and democratic goals, but in practice the highest priority usually was assigned to commercial diplomacy to fulfill administration promises to strengthen the American economy. Clinton's support for APEC was especially strong, at least during the first two years of his administration. The U.S. military in the Pacific continued the EASI process, but halted reduction of American personnel at the 100,000 level because of the dangerous situation on the Korean peninsula, particularly Pyongyang's probable nuclear weapons program. The USPACOM continued its military strategy of cooperative engagement, stressing coalition strategy with Japan, South Korea, and other allies, while attempting to reestablish ties with the Chinese People's Liberation Army severed after the 1989 Tiananmen Square incident.

President Clinton placed great emphasis on continued U.S. leadership in the region, the permanence of the U.S. military presence, and the credibility of American commitments. However, these assurances were not fully accepted by many Asians. It was reported that a number of Asian governments believed the United States to be a declining power. In part this perception was attributable to Clinton's leadership style; in larger measure it was due to the growing power of regional states. China in particular was seen as increasing its national power, a reflection of spectacular economic growth and rapid military modernization. Regional concern over Chinese intentions was heightened because of militant PRC policies toward the South China Sea and Taiwan.

The Bush and Clinton strategies toward the Asian Pacific were robust and comprehensive, with fairly close integration between global and regional strategies and between security, political, economic, and cultural aspects of U.S. policy. In the absence of a major threat to U.S. security interests, this type of comprehensive strategy should be continued, although certain weaknesses need to be corrected. The Clinton administration, for example, had difficulty assigning policy priorities in some instances -- especially in regards to China and to a lesser extent to Japan -- and in maintaining the image of the United States as regional leader. These weaknesses limited the effectiveness of U.S. strategy and contributed to a decrease in American influence in the region under President Clinton.

In addition to comprehensive strategies centered around the building of a community of market democracies in Asia, other strategic approaches might be considered by the United States as it moves toward the twenty-first century. Studies done for the USCINCPAC, for example, placed emphasis on U.S. security interests in Asia. One proposal suggested U.S. grand strategy focus on the traditional American goal of preventing the domination of Asia by any other power. In the post-Cold War era this meant collective and cooperative security arrangements, whereby the

United States would exercise global and regional leadership, but replace reliance on deterrence with a new balance of power regime in the region.

A proposed cooperative strategy for comprehensive regional security would be based on three principal components: continued American military, economic, and political engagement in the region; maintenance of the U.S.-Japan alliance; and a U.S. role as "regional leader and honest broker." The strategy suggested a comprehensive approach in which the interpretation of U.S. security would be expanded to include political, economic, and cultural elements as well as military instruments of national power and interests.

According to another study, the United States had four strategic options for the Asia-Pacific: strengthen U.S. forces in the region; continue the existing U.S. force structure but with reduced personnel and equipment; reduce the U.S. role in Asia and have other regional powers assume greater responsibility for collective security; or undertake a major retrenchment from the region. The study did not make a recommendation among these choices, but it did stress the vital importance of maintaining U.S. credibility and sustaining a favorable balance of power. Both of these essential goals could best be achieved by continuing to station forward deployed U.S. forces in the region.

A fourth USCINCPAC study noted that U.S. grand strategy was tending toward defense in combination with regional partners. This emerging strategy was based on several trends: greater emphasis on U.S. political and economic roles in regional security; the continued existence of multiple threats but the absence of urgent threats; and the absence of situations in which the United States had to act unilaterally. The size of total U.S. forces was less important than maintaining a forward presence in the Western Pacific for the purposes of deterrence and stability. In this strategy, USPACOM should place emphasis on preparing for a wide range of regional contingencies, preserving close partnerships and defense coalitions with Asian friends and allies, and maintaining a forward presence for credibility and stability but at lower cost and with reduced numbers of personnel.

Although different emphasis could be found in the strategic proposals made to the USCINCPAC, all stressed the importance of coalition defense, forward presence, U.S. leadership, deterrence, balance of power, credibility, nonproliferation, economic and political factors in post-containment strategy, and having to fulfill the U.S. military mission with fewer resources. These elements of strategy were adopted by the Bush and Clinton administrations and likely will continue to be relevant over the next decade.

Greater diversity was found in the strategic proposals of independent scholars, although they, too, emphasized the above elements of strategy. Under a strategy of convergent deterrence, for example, the United States would move from being the dominant power of the Asia-Pacific to the predominant power, while merging U.S. global deterrence strategy with more regional concerns. The long-term goal would be to replace deterrence with confidence-building measures (CBMs) as the primary means of conflict avoidance in the region. This reliance on deterrence with an eye toward increased CBM is in keeping with trends in the Asian Pacific. Deterrence no doubt will remain a key element of U.S. strategy toward Asia, but deterrence should not be the central theme of American strategy in the post-containment era because of its overemphasis on military strength.

Balance of power strategies also are relevant for Asia. Various configurations have been suggested, but the most widely discussed emphasize the U.S.-Japan-China strategic triangle and the U.S.-Japan-China-Russia strategic quadrangle. Generally, these geopolitical strategies are based on the pivotal role of U.S.-Japan relations, which is viewed in turn as being dependent on cooperative Sino-American relations. Other balance of power strategies have the United States align with Russia, Vietnam, ASEAN, or India to counter future Chinese or Japanese threats to U.S. interests in Asia.

Balance of power strategies assume that one or more of the great powers of East Asia -- China, Russia, or Japan -- will pursue hegemony at the expense of its neighbors. At the close of 1995, the nation most likely to choose this path was the People's Republic of China. Despite a policy of cooperative engagement with the PRC, Washington faced growing problems with Beijing in the areas of Taiwan, nuclear weapons testing, missile proliferation, trade, human rights, and the South China Sea. Incendiary factors included the PLA's increase of power projection capabilities with Russian and other third-country assistance, the post-Deng Xiaoping leadership transition in which contenders such as President Jiang Zemin courted conservative political backing by sounding ultra-nationalistic, and Taiwan's determination to improve its international standing in spite of PRC military threats.

As long as the United States defines its interests in terms of preventing hegemony in Asia, Washington will continue to seek a balance of power in the region. Defining and maintaining an effective balance of power will be exceedingly difficult in the post-Cold War period, however, since most Asian nations are not static powers: they are experiencing rapid economic and military growth, with an accompanying sense of national pride and destiny. The U.S. presence may be a constant in a balance of power equation, but what Asian nation is willing to accept the status quo? This is especially true in regards to China, which may become a close friend, bitter enemy, or competing rival of the United States. Moreover, American public support for a strategy of maintaining a balance of power in Asia might not be sufficient to gain the necessary resources from Congress. Further, a balance of power strategy may be outdated in today's interdependent world. Strategies centered on balance of power are too focused on military considerations and not sufficiently attuned to the economic, political, and cultural aspects of national influence, factors which are becoming more important in the post-Cold War era.

The major weakness of a balance of power strategy for the United States is that the strategy might not be viable for post-containment Asia. If Washington were unsuccessful in implementing such a strategy, then American influence in the region would decline still further, perhaps resulting in the very conditions of instability the strategy was designed to avoid. Hence, while balance of power should be part of a comprehensive U.S. strategy toward the Asian-Pacific region, it should not be the central focus of the strategy or its predominant theme.

Several strategies are possible if China emerges as a major threat to U.S. interests in Asia. These included strategies of retreat from Asia, toppling the CCP regime, containment, peaceful evolution, accommodation, confrontation, and manipulation. China, along with North Korea, are the "wild cards" in Asia's strategic environment. U.S. strategy toward the PRC is subject to rapid change, although most American planners hope that strategies of constructive engagement and peaceful evolution will work over time to moderate Beijing's policies and lead to closer Sino-American relations. At present, the United States does not want to contain China but rather to welcome it into a cooperative relationship. However, China could become a threat to U.S. interests if non-peaceful means are pursued in the Taiwan Strait and in the South China Sea and if Beijing returns to a more conservative domestic policy agenda. Washington has limited influence over these policies. Future Sino-American relations rest heavily in the hands of the Chinese.

Thus, while Sino-American relations should be an important component of U.S. strategy, it would be a mistake to base U.S. strategy either on cooperative or hostile relations with Beijing. The most reasonable approach may be a "hedge strategy" whereby the United States continues to engage China but keeps its options open in case of conflict in the Taiwan Strait or elsewhere around China's periphery. The fundamental problem in Sino-American relations is systemic: China is an expanding power seeking to change the status quo in Asia, whereas the United States is the primary defender of that status quo. Neither Beijing nor Washington is likely to change its objectives in the region, making an eventual confrontation more rather than less likely.

A similar set of strategic options can be envisioned for Japan. Under the much less probable scenario of that nation becoming an enemy of the United States, Washington could pursue strategies designed to retreat from Asia, topple a hostile government in Tokyo, contain Japanese power, peacefully evolve the Japanese system into one more compatible with U.S. interests, accommodate Japanese ambitions, militarily confront Tokyo, or attempt to manipulate Japan on a case-by-case basis.

It is far more probable that Japan will continue as the principal American ally in Asia. Thus, the focus of most strategic thought about Japan is how to redefine the U.S.-Japan security alliance to make it more relevant in the post-containment era. Some strategies would withdraw U.S. ground forces from Japan and reallocate responsibilities for security in the Western Pacific to give the United States primary responsibility for strategic nuclear defense and to give Japan responsibility for conventional defense of regional sea lanes. Other strategies would maintain U.S. forces in Japan but refocus the alliance toward North Korea and possibly China.

Under most foreseeable circumstances, Japan will continue to be an essential and dependable ally of the United States. The continuation of the alliance should be a priority in U.S. regional strategy, if only because a hostile U.S.-Japanese relationship would have severely negative repercussions for the United States and Asia. Nonetheless, the ever-present possibility of a confrontation with North Korea, uncertainties over the future course of China, and the remote possibility of a renewed Japanese threat illustrate the truism that in Asia bilateral relations and security issues can quickly outpace strategy and dominate the American policy agenda.

Collective security was a prominent feature of the Cold War and continues to be a vital element of U.S. strategy today. In fact, the post-

Cold War period has seen greater emphasis placed on collective security and other kinds of multilateralism. Many global strategies fall under the category of multilateralism. These range from efforts by the United States to mold the international system in ways serving U.S. interests, to collective security alliances to ensure world peace through cooperative engagement, to the assumption of moral responsibility to lead the world into a new world order of democracy and free markets, to unilateral restraint whereby the United States avoids intervention in world affairs to give international organizations an opportunity to act for the common good.

In Asia the United States has felt most comfortable in multilateral settings in areas of collective security and economics. U.S. collective security strategy was reflected in SEATO and in the coordination of American security alliances with various Asian states. Collective security strategy is also reflected in U.S. support for the ASEAN Regional Forum (ARF) and in suggestions for a security dialogue in Northeast Asia. Economically, the United States has been an active proponent of multilateralism throughout the postwar period. A recent example of U.S. multilateral strategy on the economic front is American encouragement of APEC as the most promising vehicle for regional economic cooperation and integration.

Multilateral strategies also have political dimensions in the Asian Pacific. Some strategists believe the United States has a moral duty to shape the new Pacific community according to democratic, free market, and collective security values. Some strategies propose the United States use the United Nations and other multilateral organizations as instruments to serve both national and international interests, as occurred with the U.N. Transitional Authority in Cambodia between 1991 and 1993.

Strategies of multilateralism, of which collective security is an important part, will probably have a prominent role in U.S. strategy through the end of the century. If the United States does not isolate itself from the rest of the international community and if it does not have the resources or the will to act unilaterally to dominate the world, then the United States will have to engage cooperatively with other nations to define and pursue common goals. The key variable is the degree of multilateralism, determined by such factors as the level of U.S. leadership and participation; and the membership, structure, agenda, and responsibility of multilateral forums and organizations. At the same time, it is clear the United States cannot depend on multilateral organizations to serve American interests. These organizations often are ineffective and sometimes pursue policies detrimental to U.S. interests. Hence, while multilateralism and collective security should be part of U.S. strategy toward Asia, they should not be predominant. The United States must maintain the ability to act unilaterally when it is in the best interests of the United States to do so.

Isolationism is a traditional element of American foreign policy. Now that the Soviet threat has dissipated, isolationists argue once again that U.S. interests are best served by concentrating on domestic problems rather than international issues. Modern isolationists generally do not favor disengagement from foreign affairs, but rather want clear priority to be given to domestic needs in the allocation of scarce resources. The subsidy of other countries at the expense of domestic programs is not acceptable in this view. Neo-isolationists find especially troublesome the huge U.S. trade deficits with Japan and China; the maintenance of a large forward American military presence in Europe and Asia; and U.S. military involvement in conflicts not directly threatening American security interests, especially when such involvement is under the control of the United Nations.

Various (and sometimes contradictory) strategies have been proposed to redirect American resources from foreign to domestic affairs. Globally, these include suggestions for greater reliance on collective security and international action to minimize American unilateral activity; strengthening the peacekeeping functions of the U.N.; cooperative security with China and Russia to place a moratorium on arms production and sale; and legislative limitations on U.S. military involvement to those situations where direct U.S. interests are threatened.

In strategy toward the Pacific Rim, isolationists argue that Asian countries are capable of taking care of themselves. The United States need not assume the burden of leadership in the region's defense, of defining and maintaining an Asian balance of power, or of tolerating huge trade deficits to preserve strategic alliances. Strategies that adopt this perspective accept the necessity of a U.S. retrenchment from the Western Pacific, perhaps to a mid-Pacific posture, and a major reduction of U.S. forces in South Korea and Japan. This retrenchment would not be due to American weakness, but rather to a strategic decision that American resources should not be wasted in overseas activities that can be handled by others.

Since isolationism has been part of the American character from the outset of the nation, there is no reason to expect that it will not continue to be a factor in U.S. strategic planning in the future. The collapse of the

158

Soviet Union resulted in the reemergence of sharp debate in the United States between isolationists and internationalists, between unilateralists and multilateralists, and between those with differing views of when and how to use American leadership and capabilities abroad. These differences may never be resolved completely, although they can be muted temporarily in the presence of a commonly perceived threat to the United States. In the absence of such a threat, isolationism will have some braking influence on American strategy toward Asia, but it should not stand in the way of U.S. involvement with the most dynamic region of the world.

Integration has emerged as a major theme in U.S. strategy since the end of the Cold War. President Bush said the challenges of integration were as formidable as those of containment; and President Clinton said integration and disintegration were two forces operating in the world, implying that he would align the United States with the former. Policy statements from both administrations frequently referred to integration as a long-term strategic goal, particularly in regards to bringing former and existing socialist countries into the international political and economic system.

Strategies of integration in the Asian Pacific focus on one or more of the following dimensions: integration of nonmarket countries into the region's political-economic systems; integration of regional economies, as through the APEC process; integration in security affairs, as through the ARF; and integration in politics, as through summit meetings between APEC leaders. To date, the most successful examples of integration are ASEAN at the subregional level and APEC at the regional economic level. ARF has had only marginal success in addressing regional security issues, and APEC summit meetings are promising but still in a stage of infancy.

Strategies of integration vary not only in terms of their dimension (economic, political, security, or cultural) but also in terms of their organizational goal (a formal institution or process of dialogue) and methods of decisionmaking (consensus or through dominant leadership). Strategies of integration are based on the assumption that greater cooperation between states strengthens the international system at the same time that it serves national interests. Since integration is congruent with trends toward greater interdependency, there is a strong possibility -- barring a war or sudden turn inward in American foreign policy -- that integration will become an essential and perhaps defining component of U.S. strategy toward the Asian Pacific.

Recommendations

Based on the foregoing analysis, the following recommendations can be made.

First, although bilateral and security issues often dominate the U.S. policy agenda toward Asia, it is vital for the United States to have a regional strategy toward the Asia-Pacific. Asia is the most dynamic region in the world and the most important trading partner of the United States. In the next century, American ties with Asia will likely become even closer. The growing importance of Asia to U.S. interests and the expanding U.S. involvement with Asia necessitate a strategic vision and plan of engagement. Strategic drift and nonengagement are not viable options for the United States in Asia.

Second, the United States needs robust and comprehensive strategies toward Asia, with close integration between global and regional objectives and tight coordination between the security, political, economic, and cultural aspects of U.S. foreign policy and national security policy in the region. Today's complex and interdependent world requires the type of comprehensive strategies adopted by Presidents Bush and Clinton. Barring the emergence of a serious threat against U.S. interests, these viable strategies should be continued. But an intellectually cogent strategy is not sufficient; in the multipolar environment of Asia the United States must work hard to ensure its commitments remain credible and to justify its continued leadership. An effective, credible strategy in Asia requires the ability to assign clear priorities when conflicts occur between various elements of U.S. strategy and policy. Since ambiguity tends to be interpreted as weakness and indecisiveness, clarity is essential in this new era.

Third, the role of the U.S. military in American strategy toward Asia remains crucial. USPACOM strategy is effective, so it should continue to include elements such as coalition defense, forward presence, deterrence, balance of power, readiness, counterproliferation, economy of force, and U.S. leadership and credibility. Greater acknowledgement needs to be given to the security roles of economic, political, and cultural interaction with Asia, as well as the promising role of integration. Deterrence at nuclear and conventional levels should remain a key element of U.S. strategy toward Asia, but cooperative engagement should continue as the central theme of American security policy.

Fourth, it remains in the U.S. interest that a favorable balance of power be maintained in Asia, one that prevents the emergence of a hostile power seeking hegemony in the region. Because of the difficulties of defining and implementing a balance of power regime in Asia, however, balance of power should not be the primary goal of U.S. strategy or its predominant theme. Both realism and idealism have crucial roles in modern American strategy toward Asia; too great of an emphasis on one or the other could prove harmful to U.S. interests.

Fifth, it would be an error to base U.S. strategy on the assumption of either cooperative or hostile relations with Beijing. The United States must keep its options open toward China, while at the same time exerting reasonable efforts to preserve a friendly relationship with the PRC and to further integrate Beijing into the Asian-Pacific community. The fundamental problem of adjusting to the expanding national power and influence of China cannot be addressed successfully until the post-Deng leadership transition is finalized and more stable PRC policies are adopted. Meanwhile, the United States must serve its own regional interests by insisting that the Taiwan and South China Sea issues be settled peacefully. If Washington allows Beijing to use force against Taipei or members of ASEAN, the United States would lose much of its remaining credibility in Asia and encourage Chinese aggression in other parts of the region.

Sixth, Japan should continue to occupy center stage in U.S. strategy toward Asia. Every effort should be made to ensure that the U.S.-Japan security alliance remains in force while trade issues are resolved in fairness to both countries. Some adjustment in the respective roles of the United States and Japan may be required, but it is vital that hostile U.S.-Japanese relations be avoided if at all possible due to the negative repercussions affecting the entire region.

Seventh, U.S. strategy toward Asia must contain strong elements of multilateralism and collective security. Such approaches are cost-effective, in conformity with Asian nationalism and maturity in international affairs, and appropriate in an era of growing interdependence in the region. At the same time, the United States cannot allow multilateral approaches to substitute for American leadership or hamper U.S. ability to act unilaterally when necessary. The actual form of multilateral cooperation can be left to circumstances, since this is an area of new growth and unexplored territory for much of Asia.

Eighth, isolationism will continue to be a factor in U.S. strategic planning in Asia, influencing such considerations as the size of the defense budget, the amount of available foreign aid, the level of political pressure exerted on Japan and China over trade surpluses, and the degree of support for American involvement in regional organizations and military operations. The debates between isolationism, internationalism, unilateralism, and multilateralism, and between politicians over how American leadership and capabilities should be employed overseas will continue unabated, barring the emergence of a significant threat to the nation.

Ninth, integration should become a more prominent feature of American strategy. Interdependence is rapidly emerging as a dominant characteristic of the Asian Pacific. At the same time, care must be exercised over how integration is defined. It should not imply the search for a supernational organization to govern affairs in the Pacific Basin; nor should it impinge on the sovereignty of Asian-Pacific states. Integration should be seen as a gradual process of increased cooperation between nation-states in economic, security, and political affairs, with greater appreciation of individual cultures. For the United States, a strategy of integration must include a strong forward deployed military presence, active political leadership, and a clear vision of the type of community being created in the region. Because integration is a comprehensive strategy drawing upon the strength of American power and the permanence of its ideals, integration is a useful descriptive term for U.S. Asian-Pacific strategy through the turn of the century.

In sum, Asia is of growing importance to the United States as various forces bring the two sides of the Pacific into closer contact and greater interdependency. At the same time, the United States faces new security dangers from countries such as China and North Korea. These trends present major challenges to Washington, which traditionally has focused on European not Asian perspectives. The strategic options discussed in these chapters are important reminders that the United States does have choices in Asia and that it can best serve its interests by carefully formulating a strategy that protects its security, expands its economic opportunities, promotes its values, and helps guide the region to a more prosperous, peaceful, and stable future.

Bibliography

Aspin, Les. *Report on the Bottom-Up Review*. Washington, D.C.: Department of Defense, October 1993.

Ball, Desmond, Richard L. Grant, and Jusuf Wanadi. *Security Cooperation in the Asia-Pacific Region*. Washington, D.C.: Center for Strategic and International Studies, 1993.

Borthwick, Mark. *Pacific Century: The Emergence of Modern Pacific Asia*. Boulder: Westview, 1992.

Bullock, Mary Brown and Robert S. Litwak, eds. *The United States and the Pacific Basin: Changing Economic and Security Relationships*. Washington: Woodrow Wilson Center Press, 1991.

Caldwell, John. *China's Conventional Military Capabilities, 1994-2004*. Washington, D.C.: Center for Strategic and International Studies, 1994.

Chang, Gordon H. *Friends and Enemies: The United States, China, and the Soviet Union*. Stanford: Stanford University Press, 1990.

Chang, Jaw-ling Joanne. *United States-China Normalization: An Evaluation of Foreign Policy Decision Making*. Baltimore: University of Maryland School of Law, 1986.

Chang, Parris H. and Martin L. Lasater, eds. *If China Crosses the Taiwan Strait: The International Response*. Lanham: University Press of America, 1993.

Chen, Jie. *Ideology in U.S. Foreign Policy: Case Studies in U.S. China Policy*. Westport: Praeger, 1992.

China: U.S. Policy Since 1945. Washington: Congressional Quarterly, Inc., 1980.

Ching, Frank. *Hong Kong and China: For Better or For Worse*. New York: China Council of the Asia Society and the Foreign Policy Association, 1985.

Chiu, Hungdah. *Constitutional Development and Reform in the Republic of China on Taiwan*. Baltimore: University of Maryland School of Law, 1993.

Clinton, Bill. *A National Security Strategy of Engagement and Enlargement*. Washington, D.C.: The White House, February 1995.

Clough, Ralph N. *Island China*. Cambridge: Harvard University Press, 1978.

_____. *Reaching Across the Taiwan Strait*. Boulder: Westview Press, 1993.

Cohen, Warren I. and Akira Iriye, eds. *The Great Powers in East Asia: 1953-1960.* New York: Columbia University Press, 1990.

Conklin, Jeffrey Scott. *Forging an East Asian Foreign Policy.* Lanham: University Press of America, 1995.

Copper, John F. *Taiwan: Nation-State or Province?* Boulder: Westview, 1990.

_____. *China Diplomacy: The Washington-Taipei-Beijing Triangle.* Boulder: Westview, 1992.

Cossa, Ralph A., ed. *Asia Pacific: Confidence and Security Building Measures.* Washington, D.C.: Center for Strategic and International Studies, 1995.

Curtis, Gerald L., ed. *Japan's Foreign Policy After the Cold War: Coping With Change.* Armonk: M.E. Sharpe, 1993.

Denoon, David B.H. *Real Reciprocity: Balancing U.S. Economic and Security Policy in the Pacific Basin.* New York: Council on Foreign Relations, 1993.

Downs, George W., ed. *Collective Security Beyond the Cold War.* Ann Arbor: University of Michigan Press, 1994.

Eminent Persons Group. *Second Report: Achieving the APEC Vision: Free and Open Trade in the Asia Pacific.* Singapore: Asia-Pacific Economic Cooperation Secretariat, August 1994.

Endress, Lee H. and others. *U.S.-Japan Security Relationship in the 1990s.* Camp H.M. Smith: USCINCPAC, Strategic Planning and Policy Directorate, August 1991.

Eulenstein, Karl and others. *USPACOM Strategy for the Year 2010.* Camp H.M. Smith: USCINCPAC, Strategic Planning and Policy Directorate, October 1989.

Fallows, James. *Looking at the Sun: The Rise of the New East Asian Economic and Political System.* New York: Pantheon, 1994.

Fu, Jen-ken. *Taiwan and the Geopolitics of the Asian-American Dilemma.* Westport: Praeger, 1992.

Gelman, Harry. *Russo-Japanese Relations and the Future of the U.S.-Japanese Alliance.* Santa Monica: Rand Corporation, 1993.

Gilbert, Stephen P. *Northeast Asia in U.S. Foreign Policy.* Beverly Hills: Sage Publications, 1979.

_____, ed. *Security in Northeast Asia: Approaching the Pacific Century.* Boulder: Westview, 1988.

Gill, R. Bates. *Chinese Arms Transfers: Purposes, Patterns, and Prospects in the New World Order.* Westport: Praeger, 1992.

_____. *The Challenge of Chinese Arms Proliferation: U.S. Policy for the 1990s.* Carlisle Barracks: U.S. Army War College, 1993.

Harding, Harry. *A Fragile Relationship: The United States and China Since 1972.* Washington: Brookings Institution, 1992.

_____ and Yuan Ming, eds. *Sino-American Relations 1945-1955: A Joint Reassessment of a Critical Decade*. Wilmington: Scholarly Resources, Inc., 1989.

Hasegawa, Tsuyoshi, Jonathan Haslam, and Andrew C. Kuchins, eds. *Russia and Japan: An Unresolved Dilemma Between Distant Neighbors*. Berkeley: University of California Press, 1993.

Hickey, Dennis Van Vranken. *United States-Taiwan Security Ties: From Cold War to Beyond Containment*. Westport: Praeger, 1994.

Houseman, Gerald L. *America and the Pacific Rim: Coming to Terms with New Realities*. Lanham: University Press of America, 1995.

Huntington, Samuel P. *The Third Wave: Democratization in the Late Twentieth Century*. Norman: University of Oklahoma Press, 1991.

Ina, Hisayoki. *A New Multilateral Agenda for the Pacific: Beyond the Bilateral Security Networks*. Washington, D.C.: John Hopkins University School of Advanced International Studies, 1993.

Iriye, Akira. *China and Japan in the Global Setting*. Cambridge: Harvard University Press, 1992.

Kahler, Miles, ed. *Beyond the Cold War in the Pacific*. San Diego: University of California Press, 1991.

Kaufmann, William W. and John D. Steinbruner. *Decisions for Defense: Prospects for a New Order*. Washington, D.C.: Brookings Institution, 1991.

Kissinger, Henry. *Diplomacy*. New York: Simon & Schuster, 1994.

Klintworth, Gary. *China's Modernization: The Strategic Implications for the Asia-Pacific Region*. Canberra: Australian Government Publishing Service, 1989.

Langdon, Frank C. and Douglas A. Ross, eds. *Superpower Maritime Strategy in the Pacific*. London: Routledge, 1990.

Lasater, Martin L. *The Taiwan Issue in Sino-American Strategic Relations*. Boulder: Westview, 1984.

_____. *Policy in Evolution: The U.S. Role in China's Reunification*. Boulder: Westview, 1988.

_____. *U.S. Interests in the New Taiwan*. Boulder: Westview, 1993.

_____. *The Changing of the Guard: President Clinton and the Security of Taiwan*. Boulder: Westview, 1995.

Lin, Chong-pin. *China's Nuclear Weapons Strategy: Tradition Within Evolution*. Lexington: Lexington Books, 1988.

Lincoln, Edward J. *Japan's New Global Role*. Washington, D.C.: Brookings Institution, 1993.

Lundestad, Geir and Odd Arne Westad. *Beyond the Cold War: New Dimensions in International Relations*. New York: Oxford University Press, 1993.

Mack, Andrew and John Ravenhill, eds. *Pacific Cooperation: Building Economic and Security Regimes in the Asia-Pacific Region.* Boulder: Westview, 1995.

Mandelbaum, Michael, ed. *The Strategic Quadrangle: Russia, China, Japan, and the United States in East Asia.* New York: Council on Foreign Relations, 1994.

Morgan, Joseph R. *Porpoises Among the Whales: Small Navies in Asia and the Pacific.* Honolulu: East-West Center, March 1994.

National Commission on America and the New World. *Changing Our Ways: America and the New World.* Washington, D.C.: Carnegie Endowment for International Peace, 1992.

National Security: Impact of China's Military Modernization in the Pacific Region. Washington, D.C.: U.S. General Accounting Office, June 1995.

Nelson, Harvey. *Power and Insecurity: Beijing, Moscow, and Washington 1949-1988.* Boulder: Lynne Rienner Publishers, 1989.

Nordlinger, Eric A. *Isolationism Reconfigured: American Foreign Policy for a New Century.* Princeton: Princeton University Press, 1995.

Pacific Business Forum. *A Business Blueprint for APEC: Strategies for Growth and Common Prosperity.* Singapore: Asia-Pacific Economic Cooperation Secretariat, October 1994.

Pollack, Jonathan D. and James A. Winnefeld. *U.S. Strategic Alternatives in a Changing Pacific.* Santa Monica: Rand Corporation, 1990.

Pye, Lucian W. *Chinese Commercial Negotiating Style.* Cambridge: Oelgeschlager, Gunn and Haig Publishers, 1982.

Robinson, Thomas W., ed. *Democracy and Development in East Asia: Taiwan, South Korea, and the Philippines.* Lanham: University Press of America, 1991.

Ross, Robert S., ed. *East Asia in Transition: Toward a New Regional Order.* Armonk: M.E. Sharpe, 1995.

Scalapino, Robert. *The Last Leninists: The Uncertain Future of Asia's Communist States.* Washington: Center for Strategic and International Studies, 1992.

Schrader, John Y. and James A. Winnefeld. *Understanding the Evolving U.S. Role in Pacific Rim Security: A Scenario-Based Analysis.* Santa Monica: Rand Corporation, 1992.

Segal, Gerald. *Defending China.* London: Oxford University Press, 1985.

Shambaugh, David. *Beautiful Imperialist: China Perceives America, 1972-1990.* Princeton: Princeton University Press, 1992.

Shearman, Peter, ed. *Russian Foreign Policy Since 1990.* Boulder: Westview, 1995.

Simon, Sheldon. *The Future of Asia-Pacific Collaboration.* Lexington: Lexington Books, 1988.

_____, ed. *East Asian Security in the Post-Cold War Era.* Armonk: M.E. Sharpe, 1993.

Smith, Tony. *America's Mission: The United States and the Worldwide Struggle for Democracy in the Twentieth Century.* Princeton: Princeton University Press, 1995.

Solomon, Richard H. *Chinese Political Negotiating Behavior: A Briefing Analysis.* Santa Monica: Rand Corporation, 1985.

Spence, Jonathan. *To Change China: Western Advisers in China, 1620-1960.* New York: Penguin Books, 1980.

Sutter, Robert G. and William R. Johnson, eds. *Taiwan in World Affairs.* Boulder: Westview, 1994.

Swanson, Bruce. *Eighth Voyage of the Dragon.* Annapolis: Naval Institute Press, 1982.

Tan, Qingshan. *The Making of U.S. China Policy: From Normalization to the Post-Cold War Era.* Boulder: Lynne Rienner Publishers, 1992.

Tow, William T. *Encountering the Dominant Player: U.S. Extended Deterrence Strategy in the Asia-Pacific.* New York: Columbia University Press, 1991.

Tucker, Nancy Bernkopf. *Taiwan, Hong Kong and the United States, 1945-1992.* New York: Twayne, 1994.

U.S. Department of Defense. *1992 Joint Military Net Assessment.* Washington, D.C.: Joint Chiefs of Staff, August 1992.

_____. *A Strategic Framework for the Asian Pacific Rim: Looking Toward the 21st Century.* Washington: U.S. Government Printing Office, 1990.

_____. *A Strategic Framework for the Asian Pacific Rim: Looking Toward the 21st Century: A Report to Congress.* Washington, D.C.: U.S. Government Printing Office, 1991.

_____. *A Strategic Framework for the Asian Pacific Rim: Report to Congress 1992.* Washington, D.C.: U.S. Government Printing Office, 1992.

_____. *United States Security Strategy for the East Asia-Pacific Region.* Washington, D.C.: U.S. Government Printing Office, 1995.

Valencia, Mark J., ed. *The Russian Far East in Transition.* Boulder: Westview, 1995.

Winnefeld, James A. and others. *A New Strategy and Fewer Forces: The Pacific Dimension.* Santa Monica: Rand Corporation, 1992.

World Bank. *The East Asian Miracle: Economic Growth and Public Policy.* New York: Oxford University Press, 1993.

Wortzel, Larry M., ed. *China's Military Modernization: International Implications.* New York: Greenwood Press, 1988.

Zhan, Jun. *Ending the Chinese Civil War: Power, Commerce, and Conciliation Between Beijing and Taipei.* New York: St. Martin's Press, 1993.

Zhao, Quansheng and Robert G. Sutter, eds. *Politics of Divided Nations: China, Korea, Germany and Vietnam.* Baltimore: University of Maryland School of Law, 1991.

About the Book and Author

As the political and economic landscape in the Asian Pacific continues to shift, the United States must reevaluate its strategy toward the region. In his timely book, Martin Lasater explores U.S. interests in Asia, considering strategies for attaining U.S. goals in the post-containment era. Citing numerous strategic options for the United States, Lasater recommends a strategy of integration as being best suited for the region through the end of the century.

Martin L. Lasater is a Visiting Research Fellow at the Gaston Sigur Center for East Asian Studies, The George Washington University, in Washington, D.C.

Index